NO STRANGERS
TO GOD

NO STRANGERS TO GOD

8 sessions on building a meaningful relationship with God

by Julie A. Gorman

VICTOR BOOKS®

A DIVISION OF SCRIPTURE PRESS PUBLICATIONS INC.
USA CANADA ENGLAND

Most Scripture quotations are from the *Holy Bible, New International Version,* ©
1973, 1978, 1984, International Bible Society. Used by permission of Zondervan
Bible Publishers.

Recommended Dewey Decimal Classification: 301.402
Suggested Subject Heading: SMALL GROUPS

Library of Congress Catalog Card Number: 91-65457
ISBN: 0-89693-018-1

1 2 3 4 5 6 7 8 9 10 Printing / Year 95 94 93 92 91

VICTOR BOOKS
A division of SP Publications, Inc.
        Wheaton, Illinois 60187

CONTENTS

PURPOSE: To build a meaningful relationship with God as we get to know Him in each session.

INTRODUCTION

No Strangers to God is for people who want to know more about the God who already knows them. An in-depth Leader's Guide is included at the back of the book with suggested time guidelines to help you structure your emphases. Each of the 8 sessions contains the following elements:

❑ **GroupSpeak**—quotes from group members that capsulize what the session is about.

❑ **Getting Acquainted**—activities or selected readings to help you begin thinking and sharing from your life and experiences about the subject of the session. Use only those options that seem appropriate for your group.

❑ **Gaining Insight**—questions and in-depth Bible study help you gain principles from Scripture for life-related application.

❑ **Growing By Doing**—an opportunity to practice the Truth learned in the Gaining Insight section.

❑ **Going The Second Mile**—a personal enrichment section for you to do on your own.

❑ **Growing As A Leader**—an additional section in the Leader's Guide for the development and assessment of leadership skills.

❑ **Pocket Principles**—brief guidelines inserted in the Leader's Guide to help the Group Leader learn small group leadership skills as needed.

❑ **Session Objectives**—goals listed in the Leader's Guide that describe what should happen in the group by the end of the session.

IS THIS YOUR FIRST SMALL GROUP?

'smol grüp: A limited number of individuals assembled together having some unifying relationship.

Kris'chən 'smol grüp: 4–12 persons who meet together on a regular basis, over a determined period of time, for the shared purpose of pursuing biblical truth. They seek to mature in Christ and become equipped to serve as His ministers in the world.

Picture Your First Small Group.

List some words that describe what you want your small group to look like.

What Kind Of Small Group Do You Have?

People form all kinds of groups based on gender, age, marital status, and so forth. There are advantages and disadvantages to each. Here are just a few:

❑ **Same Age Groups** will probably share similar needs and interests.

❑ **Intergenerational Groups** bring together people with different perspectives and life experiences.

❑ **Men's or Women's Groups** usually allow greater freedom in sharing and deal with more focused topics.

❑ **Singles or Married Groups** determine their relationship emphases based on the needs of a particular marital status.

❑ **Mixed Gender Groups (singles and/or couples)** stimulate interaction and broaden viewpoints while reflecting varied lifestyles.

However, the most important area of "alikeness" to consider when forming a group is an **agreed-on purpose.** Differences in purpose will sabotage your group and keep its members from bonding. If, for example, Mark wants to pray but not play while Jan's goal is to learn through playing, then Mark and Jan's group will probably not go anywhere. People need different groups at different times in their lives. Some groups will focus on sharing and accountability, some on work projects or service, and others on worship. *Your small group must be made up of persons who have similar goals.*

How Big Should Your Small Group Be?

The **fewest** people to include would be **4.** Accountability will be high, but absenteeism may become a problem.

The **most** to include would be **12.** But you will need to subdivide regularly into groups of 3 or 4 if you want people to feel cared for and to have time for sharing.

How Long Should You Meet?

8 Weeks gives you a start toward becoming a close community, but doesn't overburden busy schedules. Count on needing three or four weeks to develop a significant trust level. The smaller the group, the more quickly trust develops.

Weekly Meetings will establish bonding at a good pace and allow for accountability. The least you can meet and still be an effective

10

group is once a month. If you choose the latter, work at individual contact among group members between meetings.

You will need **75 minutes** to accomplish a quality meeting. The larger the size, the more time it takes to become a healthy group. Serving refreshments will add 20–30 minutes, and singing and/or prayer time, another 20–30 minutes. Your time duration may be determined by the time of day you meet and by the amount of energy members bring to the group. Better to start small and ask for more time when it is needed because of growth.

What Will Your Group Do?

To be effective, each small group meeting should include:

1. **Sharing**—You need to share who you are and what is happening in your life. This serves as a basis for relationship building and becomes a springboard for searching out scriptural truth.

2. **Scripture**—There must always be biblical input from the Lord to teach, rebuke, correct, and train in right living. Such material serves to move your group in the direction of maturity in Christ and protects from pooled ignorance and distorted introspection.

3. **Truth in practice**—It is vital to provide opportunities for *doing* the Word of God. Experiencing this within the group insures greater likelihood that insights gained will be utilized in everyday living.

Other elements your group may wish to add to these three are: a time of **worship, specific prayer** for group members, **shared projects**, a time to **socialize** and enjoy **refreshments**, and **recreation**.

ONE

Col. 2:5-7

Roots

GroupSpeak: *"I'm an only child so I never knew what it would be like to have brothers and sisters. We never had enough relatives to hold a family reunion. But when I became a member of God's family I had relatives galore. And because we know Jesus we probably have more in common than blood relatives."*

Family Roots

Several years ago Alex Haley produced a best-seller called *Roots*. This saga of black history was made into a television miniseries which captured the nation. People became interested in their own roots. There is a sense of security and continuity in looking back on generations and realizing one is a part of something larger than what is seen. Welcome to the family as we celebrate our roots!

GETTING ACQUAINTED

What's in a Family?

What do you know about your family background?

❏ Do you know which generation in your parentage first came to America?

13

❏ Do you have any significant or unusual family relatives in your line?

❏ Are you aware of the source of your name? Have others in your family held your given name?

❏ Is there a special family likeness or characteristic you know about?

If we have been born into God's family, we have another set of roots — spiritual roots.

❏ Who are persons responsible for your knowing and growing in Christ?

❏ What other factors led to your becoming a part of God's family? Groups? Circumstances? Needs?

❏ What would you include in a list of your present spiritual sources?

On the Family Roots below, write in any significant information you can recall about your heritage. Identify persons and factors in your spiritual heritage.

Twins

Find someone in this group who shares at least two things in common with you in regard to your "roots." For example, you both might come from a farm background or have grown up in the same state. After everyone has found a "roots" partner, introduce your partner and the roots you share to the rest of the group.

GAINING INSIGHT

Marker Events

There are some days that no one forgets. No one forgets his or her own birthday. When we're young we eagerly anticipate this happy event. Even when older, we are pleased when someone remembers our special day.

God's plan has always been for us to recall the days of our spiritual roots. He wants us to remember what He did so we might be adopted into His family. "For He chose us in Him before the creation of the world to be holy and blameless in His sight. In love He predestined us to be adopted as His sons through Jesus Christ, in accordance with His pleasure and will" (Ephesians 1:4-5).

As a citizen of a particular country or nationality, the history of that people is a part of your roots also. What marker events in our nation's history are still remembered today with celebrations?

Now, think back over Israel's history in the Old Testament. What marker events would you list in Israel's history?

The Exodus was one of the most important events in the Old Testament for Israel to remember. Take the Exodus Quiz and then check your answers.

Exodus Quiz
1. Where did the Exodus occur?
2. What events led up to the Exodus?
3. What two celebrations grew out of the Exodus events?
4. Who initiated the Exodus?
5. What did Israel take with them?
6. What did God provide by day and night to help Israel travel?

Answers:
1. Egypt
2. The Plagues, specifically the plague on the firstborn and Passover (Exodus 11–12)

3. The Feasts of Unleavened Bread and Passover (Exodus 12)
4. Pharaoh (Exodus 12:31)
5. Dough, silver, gold, clothing, the bones of Joseph (Exodus 12:34-36; 13:19)
6. A pillar of fire (Exodus 13:21-22)

Israel was never to forget her origin! Throughout the Old Testament over and over again the writers of Scripture refer back to the day of deliverance from slavery—the day of freedom and salvation! The remembrance of this event is so important that it is mentioned in 19 out of 39 books in the Old Testament.

Remembering was on God's mind. And He wanted the Exodus to be in Israel's memory. Her being delivered from slavery and exempted from death was worth rehearsing. Israel's spiritual roots were a priority. Her roots would remind God's people of what He had rescued them from and of what He had caused them to become.

Read the following Scripture passages.

¹⁴"This is a day you are to commemorate; for the generations to come you shall celebrate it as a festival to the LORD—a lasting ordinance. ¹⁵For seven days you are to eat bread made without yeast. On the first day remove the yeast from your houses, for whoever eats anything with yeast in it from the first day through the seventh must be cut off from Israel. ¹⁶On the first day hold a sacred assembly, and another one on the seventh day. Do no work at all on these days, except to prepare food for everyone to eat—that is all you may do. ¹⁷"Celebrate the Feast of Unleavened Bread, because it was on this very day that I brought your divisions out of Egypt. Celebrate this day as a lasting ordinance for the generations to come. . . ."

²¹Then Moses summoned all the elders of Israel and said to them, "Go at once and select the animals for your families and slaughter the Passover lamb. ²²Take a bunch of hyssop, dip it into the blood in the basin and put some of the blood on the top and on both sides of the doorframe. Not one of you shall go out the door of his house until morning. . . ."

²⁵"When you enter the land that the LORD will give you as He promised, observe this ceremony. ²⁶And when your children ask you, 'What does this ceremony mean to you?' ²⁷then tell them, 'It is the Passover sacrifice to the LORD, who passed over the houses of the Israelites in Egypt and spared our homes when He struck down the Egyptians.' " Then the people bowed down and worshiped.

Exodus 12:14-17, 21-22, 25-27

¹¹"After the LORD brings you into the land of the Canaanites and gives it to you, as He promised on oath to you and your forefathers, ¹²you are to give over to the LORD the first offspring of every womb. All the firstborn males of your livestock belong to the LORD. ¹³Redeem with a lamb every firstborn donkey, but if you do not redeem it, break its neck. Redeem every firstborn among your sons.

¹⁴"In days to come, when your son asks you, 'What does this mean?' say to him, 'With a mighty hand the LORD brought us out of Egypt, out of the land of slavery.' "

Exodus 13:11-14

¹Then Moses and the Israelites sang this song to the LORD:

"I will sing to the LORD, for He is highly exalted. The horse and its rider He has hurled into the sea. ²The LORD is my strength and my song; He has become my salvation. He is my God, and I will praise Him, my father's God, and I will exalt Him. ³The LORD is a warrior; the LORD is His name. ⁴Pharaoh's chariots and his army He has hurled into the sea. The best of Pharaoh's officers are drowned in the Red Sea. ⁵The deep waters have covered them; they sank to the depths like a stone.

⁶"Your right hand, O LORD, was majestic in power. Your right hand, O LORD, shattered the enemy. ⁷In the greatness of Your majesty You threw down those who opposed You. You unleashed Your burning anger; it consumed them like stubble. ⁸By the blast of Your nostrils the waters piled up. The surging waters stood firm like a wall; the deep waters congealed in the heart of the sea.

⁹"The enemy boasted, 'I will pursue, I will overtake them. I will divide the spoils; I will gorge myself on them. I will

draw my sword and my hand will destroy them.' ¹⁰But You blew with Your breath, and the sea covered them. They sank like lead in the mighty waters.

¹¹"Who among the gods is like You, O LORD? Who is like You—majestic in holiness, awesome in glory, working wonders? ¹²You stretched out Your right hand and the earth swallowed them.

¹³"In Your unfailing love You will lead the people You have redeemed. In Your strength You will guide them to Your holy dwelling."

Exodus 15:1-13

Based on these passages, what are some ways God wanted Israel to remember her spiritual roots of the Passover and Exodus?

In Jesus' life, the Passover rituals, recalling the Exodus, continued to play an important role. Large sections of the Gospel of John are devoted to the events of Passover week. Jesus is often noted as participating in this time of remembrance. But in the life of the early church, the Passover roots were replaced by another remembrance.

²³For I received from the Lord what I also passed on to you: The Lord Jesus, on the night He was betrayed, took bread, ²⁴and when He had given thanks, He broke it and said, "This is My body, which is for you; do this in remembrance of me." ²⁵In the same way, after supper He took the cup, saying, "This cup is the new covenant in My blood; do this, whenever you drink it, in remembrance of Me." ²⁶For whenever you eat this bread and drink this cup, you proclaim the Lord's death until He comes.

1 Corinthians 11:23-26

God wants us to regularly remember Calvary and our experience of its reality in our lives—out of acceptance by faith of

His salvation. It marks the beginning of our lives as a freed people. It recalls our roots.

Let's remember right now. Share when and how you met Jesus—your spiritual roots.

GROWING BY DOING

Celebrate!
We've looked at several different ways God established for Israel to go on remembering and celebrating her spiritual roots. What are some ways we can celebrate our spiritual history?

What ideas do you have for reflecting on and responding to what God has done?

Song of Deliverance
As a group, talk through what God has done and, using Exodus 15:1-13 as a model, compose a song of deliverance that incorporates specifics from the group's sharing of salvation histories. For example, "You delivered John from the power of sin as a young boy; Your powerful arm rescued Cynthia as a teenager in search of a purpose."

GOING THE SECOND MILE

Group Checkup
Think about the members in our group and try to remember some of the things they shared about their roots.
What's one memory this session jogged for you?

Who would list you among their spiritual roots?

What's one way you plan to keep alive the memory of your spiritual roots?

As you think about our group, what would you pray for them in this area of making God their first priority?

19

TWO

Knowing God

GroupSpeak: *"Not only did my small group give me an opportunity to get to know my relatives in the Body of Christ, but these folks helped me get to know God in a special personal way. And the closer we came to knowing God, the closer we seemed to grow to each other. It was exciting to get acquainted with God through another's perspective."* GOAL

It's Who You Know

Someone has said, "It's not *what* you know that counts, but *who* you know." No doubt about it — the *who's* that we know contribute much to our lives. Millions of greeting cards are sent every year to express that sentiment — "I'm glad I know you." While God isn't the recipient of many cards, knowing Him is a dynamic that has changed more persons' lives than any other relationship. We like to brag about knowing important or famous people. Jim Elliot, martyred missionary to the Auca Indians of South America, wrote in his journal as a college youth, "Make my way prosperous, not that I achieve high station, but that my life might be an exhibit to the value of knowing God" (*The Journals of Jim Elliot*, Revell, 1978).

Each believer's life reflects a measure of the value of knowing God. All we have to do is to ponder what would be absent from life if God were not known and the value of that relationship did not increase. Our lives bear the marks of His character. They become arenas for a show of His faithfulness, evidence of His careful planning, displays of His power, receptacles for His grace, and billboards of His goodness.

Reflect on your own life. What characteristic of God is reflected in your life? What have you reaped as a result of knowing God? How have you come to know Him better this past year? What do you know of Him now that you didn't know last year at this time? The goal of knowing Him launches us on a journey of pleasures beyond our imagination. It's incredible to think that we created beings can come to know our Creator and Lord in an intimate way.

GETTING ACQUAINTED

Letter of Recommendation

Imagine God has applied for an apartment in your building and He has listed you as a reference (someone who knows Him). Complete the following letter of recommendation for God.

Reference for God

How long have you known the above? *Since 1978*

In what context?

Circle the five most relevant qualities observed in the above.

Patient	Loyal	Does what He says	Enthusiastic
Positive	Leader	Responsible	Problem-solver
Insightful	Initiator	High Performer	Responsive
Hard Worker	Caring	Approachable	Motivator
Challenging	Creative	High Standards	Encourager

In what specific situations have you had opportunity to observe one of the above qualities in the Applicant?

Is there anything else you know about the Applicant that would help us know Him?

Now share some of your letter with the whole group.

GAINING INSIGHT

Let Me Introduce You To . . .
We come to know a person when we hear the titles by which he or she is addressed, when we observe his or her actions, and when we listen to the words he or she speaks. After the Group Leader divides the group into three teams, get with your team and complete the assignment of coming up with information about God and who He is.

Team 1
Suppose we know nothing about God—wipe the slate clean. What conclusions can we draw when we hear the names or titles by which He is known?

King	Prince of Peace	Covenant God
Counselor	Bread of Life	Good Shepherd
Rock	Lamb of God	High Priest
Truth	Hiding Place	Light of the World

Team 2
What can we learn about God from certain outstanding acts He has performed in history?

Exodus	Incarnation	Raising of Lazarus
Pentecost	Healing the Blind	Saul's Conversion
Creation	Manna	Resurrection

23

1 Pet 3:9

Team 3
What can we know about God from listening to His words?

¹But now, this is what the LORD says—He who created you, O Jacob, He who formed you, O Israel: "Fear not, for I have redeemed you; I have summoned you by name, you are Mine. ²When you pass through the waters, I will be with you; and when you pass through the rivers, they will not sweep over you. When you walk through the fire, you will not be burned; the flames will not set you ablaze."

Isaiah 43:1-2

¹⁵"Can a mother forget the baby at her breast and have no compassion on the child she has borne? Though she may forget, I will not forget you! ¹⁶See, I have engraved you on the palms of My hands; your walls are ever before Me."

Isaiah 49:15-16

¹¹"For I know the plans I have for you," declares the LORD, "plans to prosper you and not to harm you, plans to give you hope and a future. ¹²Then you will call upon Me and come and pray to Me, and I will listen to you. ¹³You will seek Me and find Me when you seek Me with all your heart."

Jeremiah 29:11-13

⁶"For I desire mercy, not sacrifice, and acknowledgment of God rather than burnt offerings."

Hosea 6:6

Now let's get together with the other teams and share our findings.

What does it mean to know God? What is the difference between knowing about God and knowing God? Perhaps the difference becomes clear when we substitute the name of a current personality. "Knowing about" George Bush is different from "knowing" George Bush.

Most of us pick up facts about God and experience God's acts as we live our lives. But knowing God intimately takes more

24

than observing His acts or collecting facts about Him. Psalm 103:7 makes an interesting distinction: "He made known His ways to Moses, His deeds to the people of Israel." To know God means going beyond His acts in history and in our lives. For example, when we know a person's character, we can predict how he or she will consistently respond in certain situations. In the same way, we can know how God will act if we understand His attributes and character.

Scripture Study
Let's look at Exodus 3 where Moses is introduced to knowing God. God's initial contact comes in the word that Moses has been chosen for the mission of releasing the Children of Israel from Egyptian bondage.

⁹"And now the cry of the Israelites has reached Me, and I have seen the way the Egyptians are oppressing them. ¹⁰So now, go. I am sending you to Pharaoh to bring My people the Israelites out of Egypt."

¹¹But Moses said to God, "Who am I, that I should go to Pharaoh and bring the Israelites out of Egypt?"

¹²And God said, "I will be with you. And this will be the sign to you that it is I who have sent you: When you have brought the people out of Egypt, you will worship God on this mountain."

¹³Moses said to God, "Suppose I go to the Israelites and say to them, 'The God of your fathers has sent me to you,' and they ask me, 'What is His name?' Then what shall I tell them?"

¹⁴God said to Moses, "I AM WHO I AM. This is what you are to say to the Israelites: 'I AM has sent me to you.' "

¹⁵God also said to Moses, "Say to the Israelites, 'The LORD, the God of your fathers — the God of Abraham, the God of Isaac and the God of Jacob — has sent me to you.' This is My name forever, the name by which I am to be remembered from generation to generation."

Exodus 3:9-15

25

What was Moses' first concern? How would you phrase Moses' question in your own words?

I am not worthy to be your spokesman who am I?

How did God respond to Moses' question?

He will be w/ Moses

What was Moses' second question to God? Had Israel really forgotten who God was—His dealings with Abraham, Isaac, and Jacob? Did they just not know what to call Him?

What three things did God reveal about Himself in verses 14-15?

Moses knew God through experiencing the reality of God in his life. Moses went through the Exodus and came to know God as a special Savior and Companion in enabling him to lead the gigantic camp-out of the Children of Israel in the wilderness. He had seen God as Provider of manna, quail, and water. He knew God as Protector and Champion as He destroyed the Egyptian army in the Red Sea. He had met God face-to-face and experienced His kindness as he received the Ten Commandments. But Moses wanted to know God *more* intimately. Read his request in the following passage.

[12]**Moses said to the LORD, "You have been telling me, 'Lead these people,' but You have not let me know whom You will send with me. You have said, 'I know you by name and you have found favor with Me.'** [13]**If You are pleased with me, teach me Your ways so I may know You and continue to find favor with You. Remember that this nation is Your people."**

¹⁴**The LORD replied, "My Presence will go with you, and I will give you rest."**

Exodus 33:12-14

What was God's response to Moses' request?

How does God's "Presence" in a situation allow us to know Him?

What would happen if instead of asking God to deliver us out of a situation, we asked Him to let us get to know Him in a new way? How would our attitude toward our circumstances change? How would our evaluation of the results change? How would our petitions change?

Let's reflect on how we get to know another individual when we go through an experience with them. How would our outlook on our day change if we saw those experiences as primarily designed for getting to know God?

How would our anticipation of each day be affected if we saw God not just helping us to get through the day successfully, but helping us to get to know Him and use His nearness to build relationships with others?

How would our small group or Sunday School/church experience be affected if we realized that everything God has designed for our learning is for the one purpose of getting to know Him more intimately?

The more we know God, the greater our enjoyment of Him. He becomes more than an emergency hot line. He becomes more than a Bestower of gifts in response to our petitions. One of the results of knowing God is a hunger to know more of Him. And there is always more of God to be known.

GROWING BY DOING

History with God

Share a time when God has revealed Himself through situations in your life. What did you come to know about God because of His going through this occasion with you? After sharing, thank God for showing you specific aspects of Himself. *He provided for us after my job loss.*

GOING THE SECOND MILE

A Changed Life

God is revealed most clearly in Scripture. As you read the following passages, consider how you know this characteristic of God in your life. Do you know a God who is as Scripture describes Him? Check the boxes beside any of the comments that closely resemble your thoughts and feelings. The answers are for your honest self-evaluation on how well you know God in your relationship and where you would like to get acquainted better.

⁹**For with You is the fountain of life; in Your light we see light.**

Psalm 36:9

☑ I'm convinced that letting God be my Light and Life through my day is the key to having the proper perspective on myself, my family, my friendships, my work, my play.

☐ My life would be more balanced and less fragmented if I daily looked to God as my Light and Life.

☐ It seems opposite of my human nature to let God be the true source of my life. Usually I feel distant from Him.

☑ If I spent time each day meditating on who God is, I would have a better grasp on how to handle my day.

¹⁵**For this is what the high and lofty One says—He who lives forever, whose name is holy: "I live in a high and holy place, but also with him who is contrite and lowly in spirit, to revive the spirit of the lowly and to revive the heart of the contrite."**

Isaiah 57:15

❑ When I have a proper view of who God is, I can look honestly at my sin and guilt. The result is my spirit and heart are lifted.

❑ It is hard for me to be humble all the time. Many times I battle pride, although when I honestly look at myself, I see I have little in myself to be proud of.

❑ I tend to be a doormat rather than be humble in the biblical expression of humility.

❑ It's hard for me to be humble and admit my sin when I don't have a proper view of how holy God is.

²⁴**"But let him who boasts boast about this: that he understands and knows Me, that I am the LORD, who exercises kindness, justice and righteousness on earth, for in these I delight," declares the LORD.**

Jeremiah 9:24

❑ God has always treated me fairly.

❑ Even when God disciplines me, He amazes me at how patient and gracious He is.

❑ Being kind and fair to others is not a high priority of mine.

❑ There are talents I have that I am rightfully proud of.

¹⁷**"Ah, Sovereign LORD, You have made the heavens and the earth by Your great power and outstretched arm. Nothing is too hard for You."**

Jeremiah 32:17

❑ Why is there so much pain and evil in the world, if nothing is too hard for God?

❑ Even though I believe God has the power to do anything, I think He has lots more important issues to be concerned about than my problems.

❑ I haven't experienced God solving my problems. I don't hear Him giving me solutions to my problems. I usually come up with solutions myself.

- ☐ Because I'm convinced God can do anything, I pray about big and small problems and ask Him for some pretty big solutions.

¹⁸You do not stay angry forever but delight to show mercy.
Micah 7:18

- ☐ Most of the time I feel God is angry with me because of my sin. It's hard for me to believe God completely forgives me.
- ☐ There is no way I can earn God's mercy. I deserve His anger instead.
- ☐ The only way I ever feel completely free of my guilt and sin is when I ask God's forgiveness and meditate on Scripture that promises His total forgiveness.
- ☐ I know God's mercy to me is immeasurable, but it's hard for me to give mercy and forgiveness to people I don't feel deserve it from me.

³But the Lord is faithful, and He will strengthen and protect you from the evil one.
2 Thessalonians 3:3

- ☐ I wish I could find one friend I could depend on all the time.
- ☐ I know I can depend on God no matter what the circumstance.
- ☐ I regularly experience God's protection of me from the evil one.
- ☐ Because I'm not a faithful friend to God, I can't expect God to be a faithful friend to me.

Planning to Know God Better
Spend some time during the next few days thinking about your relationship with God. Then complete the following statements.

A word that describes how I now feel about my relationship with God is

Something I want to know about God is

One of the results of knowing God that I would like to see in my life is

Wanting to know God means I will

What I plan to do to strengthen my relationship with God is

THREE

Being Known

GroupSpeak: *"Sometimes it's kinda scary to think that God knows you even better than you know yourself. It's scary until you remember that it was after knowing me that He said, 'I love you.' I guess everybody wants that—to be really known and still to be loved."*

The Fear of Being Known
"Don't I know you? Of course I know you! Do you know me?"

Knowing another person can range all the way from casual acquaintance to intimate interaction. Yet, we have a fear of those who have access to information about us over which we have no control. Government records, TRW reports on our credit history, and files containing personal data may reflect some of who we are, but they don't provide a holistic view of us.

Our best friends know us in a different way. Someone has said that a friend is someone who knows our most heretical thought and still loves us.

Sometimes we are surprised to discover new insights about ourselves when we thought we knew who we were. Being known is basic to trust. The more we allow another person to know, the more we trust that person. And the more we trust another person to know us, the more we want to be known. Knowing that we are known by God and still loved prompts in us a desire to know and love Him more.

GETTING ACQUAINTED

How Well Do You Know Me?

Find a partner and without discussion, put a √ by the answer you feel your partner would select for each of the following questions.

What quality do I value most in a relationship?

- ❑ loyalty
- ❑ sensitivity
- ❑ a giving nature
- ❑ honesty

What would I like for a birthday present from the person closest to me?

- ❑ $20 to purchase a gift of my choice
- ❑ A $20 gift of his or her selection
- ❑ A gift made by him or her

I just received a gift from a close friend. Although I realize my friend spent a great deal of time selecting it, I really do not like the present. What I would do is

- ❑ Take the gift back to the store without telling my friend
- ❑ Say "Thanks" and keep it without indicating my real feelings
- ❑ Tell my friend I am grateful, but I honestly don't like it

A trait in a person which annoys me most is

- ❑ Carelessness
- ❑ Dishonesty
- ❑ Ungratefulness
- ❑ Rudeness

34

If I received a large inheritance I would put it into

❑ Education
❑ Travel
❑ Personal items
❑ Investments

A personal quality I desire for my best friend to have is

❑ Ability to listen and understand
❑ Truthfulness, regardless of how much it hurts
❑ Support and belief in me

When a group is formed I am most concerned about

❑ Getting something accomplished
❑ How people feel about what is happening
❑ Keeping harmony
❑ Getting to the truth

The thing about God that I appreciate most is

❑ His availability
❑ His understanding
❑ His giving me worth
❑ His giving me hope

Now share your answers together. On the questions where you answered correctly, how did you "know" the right answers?

Best Friend
Think of one person outside this group who knows you better than anyone else—your mother, father, husband, wife, brother, sister, friend. That person can be labeled your "best friend." How would your best friend answer the following:

He or she is the kind of person who likes

He or she is the kind of person who greatly appreciates and values

He or she someday would like to

GAINING INSIGHT

If You Really Knew Me

"Hide-and-Seek" is probably one of the all-time favorites of childhood games. There is the hurried securing of yourself in a clandestine area, the approaching footsteps, the heart pounding so loud you are sure it will give you away, the awful fear that you will be found, exposed, and counted out. However, there is a contrasting feeling—the fear that you won't be found—that nobody will come, and you will be left forever imprisoned in your self-designed hideaway.

This same ambivalence invades the realm of being known by others. There is something within us that wants to reveal the real us with no facade or cover-up. At the same time, there is fear in being known. For "if you really knew me—would you still like me?"

What does it mean to you that "God knows you"? Imagine God has a personnel file with your name on it. What specific things do you see included in your file?

Scripture Study

What kinds of things does God know about us? We can catch a glimpse of God's kind of knowledge by looking at the following passage.

¹**O LORD, You have searched me and You know me. ²You know when I sit and when I rise; You perceive my thoughts from afar. ³You discern my going out and my lying down; You are familiar with all my ways. ⁴Before a word is on my tongue You know it completely, O LORD.**

⁵You hem me in—behind and before; You have laid Your hand upon me. ⁶Such knowledge is too wonderful for me, too lofty for me to attain. . . . ¹³For You created my inmost being; You knit me together in my mother's womb. ¹⁴I praise you because I am fearfully and wonderfully made; Your works are wonderful, I know that full well. ¹⁵My frame was not hidden from You when I was made in the secret place. When I was woven together in the depths of the earth, ¹⁶Your eyes saw my unformed body. All the days ordained for me were written in Your book before one of them came to be.

Psalm 139:1-6, 13-16

Circle all the things that God knows about us according to this Psalm. Then answer the following questions.

In verse 1, what does the word *search* suggest?

What do the first set of contrasts in verse 2 (*sit* and *rise*) indicate about God's knowledge?

What do you picture God observing in you today?

What realm of God's knowledge is highlighted in the second half of verse 2? How many of our personal relationships would change if people knew what we were really thinking? What changes would it make in business deals? In teaching and preaching? In parenting?

What sphere of living does verse 3 accentuate?

What does God know according to verse 4?

In verse 5, the psalmist expresses feelings that accompany the insights he is sharing. How would you identify the feeling he is conveying with his words?

According to verse 13, what does God know about our past?

Based on verse 15, what does He know about my bone and muscle structure?

An impressive feat in prenatal medicine is the perfecting of a skill to perform surgery on a fetus before it is born. What are the words used for God's action on our unborn substance?

Finally, what does verse 16 indicate about God's knowledge of us?

Nobody knows us like God does. There is nothing hidden from His sight. We are known through and through—our actions, our thoughts, our words, our lifestyles, our times.

 ## GROWING BY DOING

Knowing God Knows Me
How does God's knowledge of you make you feel?

What exactly would you say to a person who knew all this about you? Suppose you walked into the presence of a person whom you were aware knew all this about you—what statement would you make to him or her?

What was the psalmist's response in Psalm 139:6? Put this into your own words.

Read the following verses.

²³Search me, O God, and know my heart; test me and know my anxious thoughts. ²⁴See if there is any offensive way in me, and lead me in the way everlasting.
Psalm 139:23-24

How would you describe the psalmist's response to God's knowledge of him?

What does he open up to God for investigation in these verses?

Write a brief prayer, including your response to God's knowledge about you.

To a God Who Knows All about Me:

GOING THE SECOND MILE

Reflect

Take time each evening to reflect back over your day with God. Reflect not only on the events but the feelings those events caused, the motivations you recognized, and the insights you gained about who you really are. Talk over your day as you would with a best friend.

FOUR

Knowing God in Hard Times

GroupSpeak: *"Someone said, 'When you come to the end of your rope, tie a knot and hang on.' But Christians have it so much better. When you come to the end of your rope, God hangs on to you. Tough times are when you really come to know God and when you really come to know your small group that sticks with you."*

A Little Rain Must Fall

A popular and provocative best-seller by Rabbi Harold Kushner, *When Bad Things Happen to Good People* (Avon, 1983), ponders a concern wrestled with through the ages. From earliest years we are taught that if we are good, we will get a reward, Santa will come, or we will be preserved from negative consequences. We are taught that we "earn what we get."

We learn to believe that we have control over our happiness. Difficult times and hard circumstances are viewed as negative and undeserved by the person who has followed the rules.

"Why did it happen to her—she's such a good person?" we ask, as though something has gone awry in the universe—some injustice or slipup has occurred.

Scripture never promises that Christians will be exempt from difficult times. Moses chose to be mistreated along with the people of God, refusing to take advantage of his palace connections. Job became God's display piece for what it means to experience difficulties. The Apostle Paul claimed the experience of suffering as a part of knowing the living Christ. "I want to know Christ and the power of His resurrection and the fellowship of sharing in His sufferings, becoming like Him in His death" (Philippians 3:10).

While we do not pursue the hard times in our lives, we recognize that they do come. The old platitude, "Into each life some rain must fall," acknowledges that there will be occasions of stress and pain. Perhaps it is in the midst of these stretching times when we feel most vulnerable, that we come to know God and place faith in Him to a higher degree than we ever thought possible.

Faith seems to develop best in the midst of hardship, confusion, and uncertainty. The great faith chapter (Hebrews 11) notes that the saints listed there went through untold difficulties and responded by putting faith in God. Such commitment found favor in God's eyes and Hebrews 11:16 trumpets proudly that God is "not ashamed to be called their God." He wants to be known as a God who is worthy of trust and confidence in the midst of the most trying of life's circumstances. God is not a "fair-weather friend" who vanishes at the first sign of difficulty. Rather, He is committed to revealing Himself to us when it takes faith to believe He still cares.

GETTING ACQUAINTED

Your Difficult Times
Think back over your own life. What would you note as a difficult time, a time of crisis, or stressful living? Can you think of anything you learned or something that resulted from that experience?

Difficult Time   **Result**

Most times we are given no choice in the hard experiences that come to us in life. And usually everyone fears one kind more than another. In twos, share what type of "hard experience" you fear most. What do you think causes you to dread this above other things?

True, False, or Maybe

Respond to each statement by writing True, False, or Maybe.

____ We suffer difficult times because of sin in our lives. God prospers the righteous.

____ God always rescues those who are righteous in their response.

____ If we love God, everything will turn out good for us in the end.

____ We must suffer hard times so we look like Jesus.

____ We are trying to get to the place where being comfortable or not being comfortable, suffering or not suffering, going through tough times or easy times isn't the major issue.

____ God may never reveal to us the purpose of hard times.

With which of the above statements do you feel most comfortable? Why? What other questions about difficult circumstances arise in your mind?

GAINING INSIGHT

Purpose and Gain

C.S. Lewis wrote, "God whispers to us in our pleasures, speaks in our conscience, but shouts in our pains" (*The Problem of Pain*, Macmillan, 1962). Think back over the times in your life when God has been most real to you. Is it true that most of these situations have occurred during times of stress, anxiety, or suffering?

While God is often taken for granted in good times, He becomes the anchor in a time of storm—the focus of our attention. It is often here that we come to know God in a new and unique way.

We are not to crave suffering or difficult experiences—that would be masochistic and unreal. But we are not immunized against these experiences either.

43

Nowhere does Scripture suggest that God is required to give us answers or reasons for the circumstances that befall us. Yet, there are times when He reveals purposes or benefits that grow out of difficulty. Evelyn Christenson, in her powerful volume *Gaining Through Losing* (Victor, 1980), suggests the principle of God's "so that's." Along with the permitting of an unpleasant experience comes a "so that" to give it meaning and purpose. She writes, "Nothing with God is haphazard, coincidental, or happenstance. Problems in our lives do not mean that God has lost control or that He is no longer on His throne, but they give us the glorious opportunity to prove God's 'so thats'—so *that* we might gain through our losses."

Scripture Study
One of the most familiar and often quoted sections of Scripture on how to handle and profit from affliction is found in Romans 8.

[26]**In the same way, the Spirit helps us in our weakness. We do not know what we ought to pray for, but the Spirit Himself intercedes for us with groans that words cannot express.** [27]**And He who searches our hearts knows the mind of the Spirit, because the Spirit intercedes for the saints in accordance with God's will.** [28]**And we know that in all things God works for the good of those who love Him, who have been called according to His purpose.** [29]**For those God foreknew He also predestined to be conformed to the likeness of His Son, that He might be the firstborn among many brothers. . . .** [31]**What, then, shall we say in response to this? If God is for us, who can be against us? . . .** [33]**Who will bring any charge against those whom God has chosen? It is God who justifies. . . .** [35]**Who shall separate us from the love of Christ? Shall trouble or hardship or persecution or famine or nakedness or danger or sword? . . .**

[37]**No, in all these things we are more than conquerors through Him who loved us.** [38]**For I am convinced that neither death nor life, neither angels nor demons, neither the present nor the future, nor any powers,** [39]**neither height nor depth, nor anything else in all creation, will be able to separate us from the love of God that is in Christ Jesus our Lord.**
Romans 8:26-29, 31, 33, 37-39

Notice how verse 28 begins with three powerful words—
"And we know." To get the full impact of the word *know*,
let's substitute some words. For instance, the verse doesn't
begin with "And we wish." What else does it not say?

In this case, *know* means "absolute, unshakable confidence."
When you have absolute confidence in a truth, you act on it,
count on it, depend on it. What happens when we face life's
experiences with this kind of confident knowledge?

This confident kind of knowledge contrasts sharply to what
the author has just written in verse 26. What do we not know
in the midst of our weakened condition?

Why do you think we feel this inadequacy and confusion?

When we realize that we are in this state of helplessness and
are seemingly unable to pray effectively, what encouragements does verse 28 provide? In what ways does knowing
that "God works" give us courage to go on?

Notice the second major phrase of verse 28, "God works." It
is God who controls. He is in charge, not a helpless victim.
He knows what true good is. How do the last four words of
verse 28 give direction to His "working"?

How would you explain the phrase "God works for the
good"? Verse 28 does not say "all things are good." Nor does
it say "we see all things working together for good." Often,

45

because we cannot see this happening, we begin to doubt it. We see only what is around us and that sight is limited. In speaking on Romans 8, Charles Swindoll gave an excellent illustration of our perspective compared to God's.

> "I think of it as though we are little fleas in the carpet. The carpet is multicolored but that little flea, when he's on red, sees nothing but red. If you were to ask him what the carpet's like, he would say, "it's a red carpet," until suddenly he hops and he goes over and lands on green. Suddenly his once red carpet is now green and he would swear to the fact that it is green and it will be forever green until he jumps on to yellow and then everything is yellow. We see the immediate, God sees the total picture, the whole ultimate scene" (First Evangelical Free Church, Fullerton, California, 1976).

What kinds of feelings are cultivated in you when you realize that God's knowledge and perspective are far beyond your own?

God's purpose is ultimate good. There is no difficulty, however small, but what it can be redeemed for ultimate good—Satan's strongest attacks against us, the harshest inadequacies of our bodies, the world's most despicable treatment of us, the most tragic of circumstances—all will be transformed into goodness by the One who purposes good, not evil.

According to verse 29, what is one of those "good" results that God purposes?

Because of what Paul knew of his God, his confidence grew. What benefits of that confidence did Paul declare in verses 33-35?

Let's list our own possibilities for difficult circumstances, paralleling those Paul lists.

46

GROWING BY DOING

Questions for Reflection

Think through the following questions for reflection.

- ❑ What is a difficulty you face right now?
- ❑ What questions are you asking?
- ❑ What are you praying?
- ❑ Which truths help you deal with this difficulty?

Now divide into pairs and share together in two ways:

- ❑ How has the love of God brought you through a difficult situation?
- ❑ How does knowing God equip you to face a difficult situation right now?

Spend time praying for one another and supporting one another.

GOING THE SECOND MILE

Group Checkup

Who is someone who could gain from your experience of difficult times?

How can you care for someone in the group who is experiencing difficult circumstances right now?

How is another caring for you?

Write a prayer to God regarding the stressful circumstance you noted above. Then write out what you think God's answer would be to you.

Dear God:

FIVE

Knowing God Through His Will

GroupSpeak: *"When I became a Christian, God's will seemed rather spooky and hard to discover. But hearing from other believers about how they made choices in their lives gave me a whole new perspective on what it means to know the will of God."*

Cutting Through the Misconceptions

When faced with decisions, when responsibility weighs heavily upon us, when fearful of consequences—we long for someone or something to tell us what to do. We grasp at gaining meaning for the future. We would rejoice over handwriting in the sky.

Some of us revert to putting our trust in a power outside ourselves—even an unreliable power such as the odds in the flip of a coin. Others search the patterns of the stars, the wisdom of the latest guru, or the evidence from parapsychology. Something bigger than us must be in control—must have more complete insight—must be able to save us from pain, grief, and wrong turns with their resulting pressures.

Christians are not immune from this hunger to gain special insight into the unknown. As long as we think of the will of God as hidden truth guarded by restrictive boundaries and shared with only a select few, we will seek a mysterious package which God dangles just out of reach. In reality, God has revealed to us in the multitude of verses, principles, and records of people in Scripture a clear unveiling of what He wants. It is in knowing God that we come to know His will and what He desires.

The will of God has become the subject of much misconception. It has been questioned and twisted so that many give up the pursuit as being too exhausting and confusing to be worth the effort. Witness the kinds of questions that trouble people on this issue.

❑ Does God really care what choices I make?
❑ How can a person discover the will of God?
❑ Does the listing of pros and cons reveal the will of God?
❑ Can I trust my natural desires, inclinations, and common sense?
❑ Is it possible to know God's will beforehand or only in hindsight?
❑ Does God give specifics?
❑ Does God still reveal His will as He did in Bible times?
❑ Will knowing God's will keep us from making mistakes and suffering?
❑ How do you respond to a person who says, "God told me to . . ."?
❑ Is it easier to know God's will when you get older?

This session will help us cut through the misconceptions and come to know God's will through knowing Him.

GETTING ACQUAINTED

Hungry for the Future
People are hungry to know the future—to know what they should or should not be doing. What are all the ways people seek guidance today—methods they use to discover what they should do?

Agree/Disagree

Discuss whether you agree or disagree with each of the following statements.

☐ God reveals His will one step at a time.
☐ Everybody can know and do the will of God.
☐ To know the will of God is to find out where He wants us to go or what He wants us to do.
☐ The will of God may change. ?
☐ We should check every act to know whether it is God's will for us.
☐ In a decision, the harder of the two choices is usually God's will.

GAINING INSIGHT

Finding God's Will

Knowing God's will is probably one of the subjects of most concern (and most confusion!) to conscientious Christians. Some make it a "magical," almost superstitious experience.

☐ "If David calls me tonight, then he must be the one I am to marry."
☐ "If I get an IRS refund check, then I must be supposed to buy that car."

For some, finding God's will is like being a participant on a game show—"God has hidden the right answer behind a particular door. I just have to guess the right door." Or, as someone put it, we see God as a divine Easter bunny who has hidden our eggs. We have the task of hunting in the right places and finding them, while God smugly watches and spurs us on with "You're getting warmer," as we near the right hiding place.

We know from Scripture that God has a will. We also know that He wills certain things to take place. In Hebrews we learn that when Christ came into the world, He said, "I have come to do Your will, O God" (Hebrews 10:7).

Many of our misconceptions about God's will go back to how well we "know" God. Because we have an inaccurate view of

51

who God is, we have difficulty finding His will. Let's look at some statements—not to see if they are correct or incorrect—but to discover what view of God is reflected by each statement.

❑ We should put out a "fleece" to find God's will.
❑ If we miss the will of God, we must live with second best.
❑ If we ask for God's will, He will probably send us to Africa, make us stay single, ask us to give up our new car, etc.
❑ If it is God's will, it will fall in place and everything will go smoothly.

What ideas about God might be held by a person making each of these statements?

Let's look at four principles regarding God's will and then talk about some areas where we focus on it in our lives.

Principle #1
Knowing God Is Key to Knowing His Will
If someone said, "Let's all do what Henri Hirchenberger wants," our response would probably be, "Who is Henri Hirchenberger?" In the same way, when we want to do what God wants, we may have to ask, "Who is God?" While we can never know God completely, the more we know God, the more likely we are to know His will.

Let's look at a passage of Scripture that underscores this principle.

²⁴The Jews gathered around Him, saying, "How long will You keep us in suspense? If You are the Christ, tell us plainly."

²⁵Jesus answered, "I did tell you, but you do not believe. The miracles I do in My Father's name speak for Me, ²⁶but you do not believe because you are not My sheep. ²⁷My sheep listen to My voice; I know them, and they follow Me." . . .

³⁷"Do not believe Me unless I do what My Father does. ³⁸But if I do it, even though you do not believe Me, believe the

miracles, that you may know and understand that the Father is in Me, and I in the Father."

John 10:24-27, 37-38

What did the Jews want to know?

What was Jesus' response to their request?

What does He suggest as the reason why God's will was hidden from them?

What was the purpose of the wonders He performed?

Why do you think it was difficult for the Jews to see the truth the miracles were attempting to portray?

In the chapter just previous to this, the Pharisees gave evidence of being blind to the truth of God because of refusing to know God.

¹As He went along, He saw a man blind from birth. ²His disciples asked Him, "Rabbi, who sinned, this man or his parents, that he was born blind?"

³"Neither this man nor his parents sinned," said Jesus, "but this happened so that the work of God might be displayed in his life. ⁴As long as it is day, we must do the work of Him who sent Me. Night is coming, when no one can work. ⁵While I am in the world, I am the light of the world."

⁶Having said this, He spit on the ground, made some mud with the saliva, and put it on the man's eyes. ⁷"Go," He

53

told him, "wash in the Pool of Siloam" (this word means Sent). So the man went and washed, and came home seeing.

⁸His neighbors and those who had formerly seen him begging asked, "Isn't this the same man who used to sit and beg?" ⁹Some claimed that he was.

Others said, "No, he only looks like him."

But he himself insisted, "I am the man."

¹⁰"How then were your eyes opened?" they demanded.

¹¹He replied, "The man they call Jesus made some mud and put it on my eyes. He told me to go to Siloam and wash. So I went and washed, and then I could see."

¹²"Where is this man?" they asked him.

"I don't know," he said.

¹³They brought to the Pharisees the man who had been blind. ¹⁴Now the day on which Jesus had made the mud and opened the man's eyes was a Sabbath. ¹⁵Therefore the Pharisees also asked him how he had received his sight. "He put mud on my eyes," the man replied, "and I washed, and now I see."

¹⁶Some of the Pharisees said, "This man is not from God, for He does not keep the Sabbath."

But others asked, "How can a sinner do such miraculous signs?" So they were divided. . . .

²⁴A second time they summoned the man who had been blind. "Give glory to God," they said. "We know this man is a sinner."

²⁵He [the man born blind] replied, "Whether He is a sinner or not, I don't know. One thing I do know. I was blind but now I see!"

²⁶Then they asked him, "What did He do to you? How did He open your eyes?"

²⁷He answered, "I have told you already and you did not listen. Why do you want to hear it again? Do you want to become His disciples, too?"

²⁸Then they hurled insults at him and said, "You are this fellow's disciple! We are disciples of Moses! ²⁹We know that God spoke to Moses, but as for this fellow, we don't even know where He comes from."

³⁰The man answered, "Now that is remarkable! You don't know where He comes from, yet He opened my eyes. ³¹We know that God does not listen to sinners. He listens to the godly man who does His will. ³²Nobody has ever heard of opening the eyes of a man born blind. ³³If this man were not from God, He could do nothing."

³⁴To this they replied, "You were steeped in sin at birth; how dare you lecture us!" And they threw him out.

John 9:1-16, 24-34

In verse 16, we see that the religious leaders revealed their limited understanding of who Jesus was. What kept them from believing and perceiving truth?

When they questioned the formerly blind man a second time, what conclusions did they come to?

How does this incident in John 9 illustrate what Jesus declared in John 10:25-26?

Often, the circumstances God allows in our lives are to bring us to know Him, which is the beginning of knowing His will. The better we know God, the more we can accept His will.

55

He is not always ready to show us what to do, but He is always ready to show us who He is.

Principle #2
It Is God's Nature to Reveal Himself and His Will

God is not a God who hides Himself. He is a God who wants to be found. When a parent plays "Hide-And-Seek" with a young child, he or she plays to be found. God longs that we find Him. Read the following passage to see how it suggests that God's nature is to reveal Himself.

⁸Philip said, "Lord, show us the Father and that will be enough for us."

⁹Jesus answered: "Don't you know Me, Philip, even after I have been among you such a long time? Anyone who has seen Me has seen the Father. How can you say, 'Show us the Father'? ¹⁰Don't you believe that I am in the Father, and that the Father is in Me? The words I say to you are not just My own. Rather, it is the Father, living in Me, who is doing His work. ¹¹Believe in Me when I say that I am in the Father and the Father is in Me; or at least believe on the evidence of the miracles themselves."

John 14:8-11

What evidence do you find that God wants us to know Him?

God not only reveals Himself, but He also discloses His will. Notice the two commands Paul gives the Ephesians: "Therefore do not be foolish, but understand what the Lord's will is" (Ephesians 5:17). God and His will are revealed.

Principle #3
Knowing God's Principles Helps Us Know God's Will

In Hebrews, the writer speaks of our being equipped "with everything good for doing His will," and that God will "work in us what is pleasing to Him" (Hebrews 13:21). What is the implication here regarding God's will?

Read the following passages.

¹⁹Jesus gave them this answer: "I tell you the truth, the Son can do nothing by Himself; He can do only what He sees His Father doing, because whatever the Father does the Son also does. . . .

³⁰"By Myself I can do nothing; I judge only as I hear, and My judgment is just, for I seek not to please Myself but Him who sent Me."
John 5:19, 30

²⁸So Jesus said, "When you have lifted up the Son of Man, then you will know that I am the one I claim to be, and that I do nothing on My own but speak just what the Father has taught Me. ²⁹The one who sent Me is with Me; He has not left Me alone, for I always do what pleases Him."
John 8:28-29

⁴⁹"For I did not speak of My own accord, but the Father who sent Me commanded Me what to say and how to say it."
John 12:49

When Jesus came into this world He announced that He came to do God's will. How did He know what to do?

Many times we agonize over knowing the will of God because we don't know what the Word of God says in principle. When we know what God's basic guidelines are, we are channeled in the right direction. Nothing can be the will of God that is contrary to the Word of God. Once the question, "Is it in agreement with the Word of God?" has been settled, it doesn't matter what we decide to be or do or where we decide to go.

Principle #4
Application of God's Principles Will Lead Us into Doing God's Will
Let's form some guidelines for doing the will of God. Read the following passages and answer the questions.

57

17"If anyone chooses to do God's will, he will find out whether My teaching comes from God or whether I speak on My own."

John 7:17

What does this verse tell us about doing God's will?

11"'For I know the plans I have for you," declares the LORD, "plans to prosper you and not to harm you, plans to give you hope and a future."

Jeremiah 29:11

What does this verse tell us about God's plans?

1Therefore, I urge you, brothers, in view of God's mercy, to offer your bodies as living sacrifices, holy and pleasing to God—this is your spiritual act of worship. 2Do not conform any longer to the pattern of this world, but be transformed by the renewing of your mind. Then you will be able to test and approve what God's will is—His good, pleasing and perfect will.

Romans 12:1-2

What guidelines do you find in these verses?

8For you were once darkness, but now you are light in the Lord. Live as children of light 9(for the fruit of the light consists in all goodness, righteousness and truth) 10and find out what pleases the Lord.

Ephesians 5:8-10

What principle do you find in this passage?

¹⁴This is the confidence we have in approaching God: that if we ask anything according to His will, He hears us.

1 John 5:14

What realm does the will of God impact in this verse?

GROWING BY DOING

God's Will Now

Let's divide into groups of three or four to share which of the above guidelines affect our lives in doing the will of God. For instance, in knowing the will of God right now ...

❑ What in the Word of God helps you know His will?
❑ What do you know about God that assures you as you think of doing His will?
❑ Where do you need to be convinced that He is trustworthy?
❑ Where do you need to believe God?
❑ What action do you need to take to begin acting on the principles of God?

GOING THE SECOND MILE

A Person After God's Own Heart

What is an area of your life where you would like to know God's will?

Read 1 Samuel 17:32-47 to see how David knew and acted on the will of God.

SIX

Knowing God Through the Sacraments

GroupSpeak: *"For years I never really understood the significance of Baptism and the Lord's Supper. It was just something you did as a Christian."*

A Common Heritage

A newborn baby has more to learn than words and phrases. There is a whole world of meaningful messages wrapped up in the symbolic gestures we share with one another. What message do each of these symbolic acts convey?

Saluting a flag   Adding your signature to a contract
Exchanging rings   Raising of eyebrows
Lighting candles   Celebrating Memorial Day

In the Scriptures, God's people have a rich history of finding symbolic meaning in certain events. Both the ark and the Exodus depicted God's salvation of His people. Anointment with oil symbolized a setting apart for a special mission. A cup running over suggested great blessing, and the building of stone monuments signified a place where a momentous event occurred.

There are two specific acts in which God has commanded all His people to participate. Both Baptism and the Lord's Supper are rich symbols of the Christian's relationship to God

61

and to the body of Christ. And by participating in these acts, we can come to know God better and be bound together with others in the body of Christ.

GETTING ACQUAINTED

Test Yourself

How much do you know about the sacraments? Test yourself on the following.

❑ Where in the New Testament would you look for information on the Lord's Supper?

❑ Which of these time frames is mentioned in the Lord's Supper?
     Past?   Present?   Future?

❑ To which Old Testament feast is the Lord's Supper related?

❑ Why is the word *Communion* used to describe the Lord's Supper in the New Testament? Fellowship

❑ Who baptized Jesus? Why was He baptized? God Commanded it

❑ Did Jesus give thanks for each of the elements in the Last Supper? yes

❑ Did Jesus eat and drink of the bread and the cup at the Last Supper? yes

❑ Was singing a hymn part of the Last Supper? yes

❑ Did Jesus baptize others? No

Share your answers with the group.

GAINING INSIGHT

Symbolic Acts

Imagine a visitor from an uncivilized tribe attending a baseball game for the first time. What would seem strange to him or her? What questions would he or she ask?

Now imagine an unbeliever observing Communion or a Baptismal service. What would seem strange? What questions would he or she ask?

The story is told of an Indian guru who gathered his followers around him one day during meditation and was interrupted by the arrival of a cat. The animal rubbed and purred and became a general distraction to the time of meditation. The guru slipped a piece of string from his clothing and carefully tied the cat to a stick to restrain it. Soon, however, the tying of a cat to a stick became something of a ritual for the whole group. Each disciple developed more elaborate ways to restrain the cat. In the course of time, the group lost its meditative nature and instead became known as a society for the prevention of cruelty to cats. In reality, it had lost its authentic character.

This session gives us the opportunity to reflect anew on the two experiences of Baptism and Communion and to discover afresh their authentic character. What did God originally intend in the establishment of these two acts? What do they reveal to us of God?

Baptism

In the early church there was an immediate response of Baptism when a person came to faith in Christ. Jesus Himself experienced Baptism. Let's read that account.

¹In those days John the Baptist came, preaching in the Desert of Judea ²and saying, "Repent, for the kingdom of heaven is near." . . . ⁶Confessing their sins, they were baptized by him in the Jordan River. . . . ¹³Then Jesus came from Galilee to the Jordan to be baptized by John. ¹⁴But John tried to deter Him, saying, "I need to be baptized by You, and do You come to me?" ¹⁵Jesus replied, "Let it be so now; it is proper for us to do this to fulfill all righteousness." Then John consented. ¹⁶As soon as Jesus was baptized, He went up out of the water. At that moment heaven was opened, and He saw the Spirit of God descending like a dove and lighting on Him. ¹⁷And a voice from heaven said, "This is My Son, whom I love; with Him I am well pleased."

Matthew 3:1-2, 6, 13-17

What was required of those whom John baptized?

Why was John hesitant to baptize Jesus?

Why then was Jesus baptized? To full fill all righteousness

Read the following passage to discover the importance Baptism has for us.

> ³Or don't you know that all of us who were baptized into Christ Jesus were baptized into His death? ⁴We were therefore buried with Him through baptism into death in order that, just as Christ was raised from the dead through the glory of the Father, we too may live a new life.
>
> **Romans 6:3-4**

What does Baptism symbolize for us?

Now, read this passage to get a better understanding of what happens during Baptism.

> ¹¹In Him you were also circumcised, in the putting off of the sinful nature, not with a circumcision done by the hands of men but with the circumcision done by Christ, ¹²having been buried with Him in baptism and raised with Him through your faith in the power of God, who raised Him from the dead.
>
> **Colossians 2:11-12**

What was the sign of being a part of God's chosen people in the Old Testament?

What is the sign of being a part of God's chosen people today?

What do we learn about God in the requirement of Baptism?

Communion

Suppose the only section of Scripture you had ever read is the following passage on the Lord's Supper. What would you know of God just from this celebration of the Lord's Supper?

¹⁴When the hour came, Jesus and His apostles reclined at the table. ¹⁵And He said to them, "I have eagerly desired to eat this Passover with you before I suffer. ¹⁶For I tell you, I will not eat it again until it finds fulfillment in the kingdom of God."

¹⁷After taking the cup, He gave thanks and said, "Take this and divide it among you. ¹⁸For I tell you I will not drink again of the fruit of the vine until the kingdom of God comes."

¹⁹And He took bread, gave thanks and broke it, and gave it to them, saying, "This is My body given for you; do this in remembrance of Me."

²⁰In the same way, after the supper He took the cup, saying, "This cup is the new covenant in My blood, which is poured out for you."

Luke 22:14-20

List some things you can know about God from reading this passage.

Why do you think God chose a meal instead of a message to remind us of vital truths that He didn't want us to forget?

Symbols

Communion is communication. What is God communicating to us through Communion?

Let's look at Paul's account of the Lord's Supper.

²³For I received from the Lord what I also passed on to you: The Lord Jesus, on the night He was betrayed, took bread, ²⁴and when He had given thanks, He broke it and said,

"This is My body, which is for you; do this in remembrance of Me." ²⁵In the same way, after supper He took the cup, saying, "This cup is the new covenant in My blood; do this, whenever you drink it, in remembrance of Me." ²⁶For whenever you eat this bread and drink this cup, you proclaim the Lord's death until He comes.

²⁷Therefore, whoever eats the bread or drinks the cup of the Lord in an unworthy manner will be guilty of sinning against the body and blood of the Lord. ²⁸A man ought to examine himself before he eats of the bread and drinks of the cup. ²⁹For anyone who eats and drinks without recognizing the body of the Lord eats and drinks judgment on himself. ³⁰That is why many among you are weak and sick, and a number of you have fallen asleep.

1 Corinthians 11:23-30

Where did Paul get his instructions about the Lord's Supper?

The Old Testament counterpart for Baptism is circumcision. In what Old Testament celebration does Communion have its roots?

After Jesus took the unleavened bread, what two acts did He perform?

Why was the bread unleavened? What does leaven stand for in Scripture? How then is Christ like this unleavened bread?

How are we to receive the Lord's Supper? How are we to "remember Jesus"?

Let's just take a minute to share on this. What kind of things are you remembering about Jesus as you think about Him right now?

The next act of Jesus reminds us of His promise. What does the cup symbolize?

Finally, this celebration of the Lord's Supper is a preaching service. Who are the preachers and what is proclaimed according to verse 26?

GROWING BY DOING

Looking Back
Let's look back and remember God's mercy and give thanks. Share one way you have been reminded of His mercy in this session.

Looking In
Now let's look in. Paul said we are to examine ourselves before we partake. Just as there was to be no leaven in the bread, there is to be no sin in us. Take a few minutes to examine yourself and confess your sins to God.

Looking Around
Now let's look around and enjoy the fellowship of God's family. As we share the bread together, let's think of ways in which we are united.

Looking Forward
Finally, as we take the cup, let's look forward and anticipate. Jesus ended the Supper with a vow. He said, "I'll not drink of this Passover cup again until the day when I drink it with you in the kingdom of God." Think of it—some day we will drink this with Jesus. He'll say "take this cup" and we'll feast together with Him at a great dinner in our honor and His.

GOING THE SECOND MILE

Hymn Study
Locate a copy of the hymn, "And Can It Be." Charles Wesley wrote this hymn as an expression of his awe at the privilege of being a recipient of the love of the Savior. As you reflect on the words, which phrases particularly stimulate you to praise?

SEVEN

Knowing God— A Means to Spiritual Growth

GroupSpeak: *"I'm convinced that wherever you find a Christian who is growing, you will find a group of people helping that person expand his or her concept of God. That's always been true in my life."*

Evidence of Growth

Remember how excited you got as a child when you noticed evidence of physical growth? For some, that memory is connected to the ascending measurement marks on the wall where they stood tall while a parent drew a line to mark the top of their heads. For others, it was the cry of dismay from a mother who noted with alarm that last year's clothing no longer fit. The pictorial evidence supports our changing features—the toothless grin on our first-grade picture, the thinning face and gangly limbs as we moved through the ranks of grade school.

We should get excited about growth, for where there's growth, there's life. Growth happens when conditions such as nourishment and care are present. Growing in the spiritual dimension is nourished by knowing God more intimately. While growth cannot be forced, it can be fostered, and that's the focus of this session's small group experience.

GETTING ACQUAINTED

Growth Report

What is the first answer that comes to your mind for the following questions?

- ☐ Who is a person who has helped you grow?
- ☐ What is an experience or situation that caused growth in you?
- ☐ What is a new insight you have recently gained?
- ☐ What new skill have you acquired—something you now know how to do which formerly you were unable to do?
- ☐ What change of attitude have you observed in yourself?
- ☐ How have you grown as a result of being together with the members of our group?

Spiritual Growth Chart

Use the time line below to chart your spiritual growth since becoming a Christian. Show progressions and dips, noting with a symbol or word any events, people, or other causes for peaks or valleys. Then share your chart with other group members.

GAINING INSIGHT

The Growth Cycle

The old nursery rhyme goes: "Mary, Mary, quite contrary, How does your garden grow?" And the improbable answer is given, "With silver bells, and cockle shells, and pretty maids all in a row."

70

We chuckle at the ridiculousness of this verse, for any backyard gardener knows too well what makes a garden grow, and it has nothing to do with shells, bells, or lined up maids (unless they are hoeing and spraying their rows).

What gardener expects his or her garden plot to yield a harvest merely by perusing a seed catalog, choosing bulbs and plants, and then settling back to watch and wait? Nowadays, there is the soil enrichment, the chemical balance, the watering by timer, the covering from heat, the dusting for blight, the protection from snails and other rabid vermin, the continual pulling of weeds, and the coaxing into harvest with regularized fertilizing. Then, at long last, the blooms arrive and are worth their weight in gold.

In the same naive way, we sometimes think Christians grow without any intentional action, without any focus and planning, doubts, hard work, or pain. Spiritual growth is a process that involves knowing God. Which do you think comes first: knowing God or growth?

Actually each precedes the other. We must know God to grow but, as we grow, we come to know God. In his letter to the Colossians, Paul gave us an amazing growth cycle that pictures what must be going on in us if we are to continue growing in knowing God.

Let's read Colossians 1:9-12, looking for the growth steps Paul suggests for the Colossian believers.

⁹For this reason, since the day we heard about you, we have not stopped praying for you and asking God to fill you with the knowledge of His will through all spiritual wisdom and understanding. ¹⁰And we pray this in order that you may live a life worthy of the Lord and may please Him in every way: bearing fruit in every good work, growing in the knowledge of God, ¹¹being strengthened with all power according to His glorious might so that you may have great endurance and patience, and joyfully ¹²giving thanks to the Father, who has qualified you to share in the inheritance of the saints in the kingdom of light.

Colossians 1:9-12

71

What format did Paul use to communicate these growth steps?

What was the first thing he prayed for the Colossians?

Where would we expect to find this revelation of God's thoughts and plans and decisions He has willed?

According to verse 9, how are we to know God's will?

Can you think of some Bible characters who knew the Word of God on an intellectual level, but didn't relate it to their lives?

Sometimes we can more easily see how somebody else could apply Scripture in his or her life. It's harder to see how we can change and respond to God in some way in our lives. Paul prayed that the Colossians would have wisdom and an understanding of the Word of God so they could apply it in their particular situations.

But it's not enough to come up with how the truth of God can be applied to your life. What else did Paul pray for?

How could you rephrase "live a life worthy of the Lord, pleasing Him"?

According to this passage, what two things happen as a result of actually doing the Word of God in our lives?

GROWING BY DOING

Growing in Knowing

Responding to the Word of God in our everyday situations leads to a growing knowledge of God. This is how we grow in knowing Him: (1) Know what His Word says; (2) Understand its meaning; (3) See how it could work in our lives right now; (4) Start doing it.

Let's try it. We can put this process into practice right now. Read the following passage and apply these four steps as you work through the passage together.

¹At Caesarea there was a man named Cornelius, a centurion in what was known as the Italian Regiment. ²He and all his family were devout and God-fearing; he gave generously to those in need and prayed to God regularly. ³One day at about three in the afternoon he had a vision. He distinctly saw an angel of God, who came to him and said, "Cornelius!"

⁴Cornelius stared at him in fear. "What is it, Lord?" he asked.

The angel answered, "Your prayers and gifts to the poor have come up as a memorial offering before God. ⁵Now send men to Joppa to bring back a man named Simon who is called Peter. ⁶He is staying with Simon the tanner, whose house is by the sea."

⁷When the angel who spoke to him had gone, Cornelius called two of his servants and a devout soldier who was one of his attendants. ⁸He told them everything that had happened and sent them to Joppa.

⁹About noon the following day as they were on their journey and approaching the city, Peter went up on the roof

to pray. ¹⁰He became hungry and wanted something to eat, and while the meal was being prepared, he fell into a trance. ¹¹He saw heaven opened and something like a large sheet being let down to earth by its four corners. ¹²It contained all kinds of four-footed animals, as well as reptiles of the earth and birds of the air. ¹³Then a voice told him, "Get up, Peter. Kill and eat."

¹⁴"Surely not, Lord!" Peter replied. "I have never eaten anything impure or unclean."

¹⁵The voice spoke to him a second time, "Do not call anything impure that God has made clean."

¹⁶This happened three times, and immediately the sheet was taken back to heaven.

¹⁷While Peter was wondering about the meaning of the vision, the men sent by Cornelius found out where Simon's house was and stopped at the gate. ¹⁸They called out, asking if Simon who was known as Peter was staying there.

¹⁹While Peter was still thinking about the vision, the Spirit said to him, "Simon, three men are looking for you. ²⁰So get up and go downstairs. Do not hesitate to go with them, for I have sent them."

²¹Peter went down and said to the men, "I'm the one you're looking for. Why have you come?"

²²The men replied, "We have come from Cornelius the centurion. He is a righteous and God-fearing man, who is respected by all the Jewish people. A holy angel told him to have you come to his house so that he could hear what you have to say." ²³Then Peter invited the men into the house to be his guests.

The next day Peter started out with them, and some of the brothers from Joppa went along. ²⁴The following day he arrived in Caesarea. Cornelius was expecting them and had called together his relatives and close friends. ²⁵As Peter entered the house, Cornelius met him and fell at his feet in reverence. ²⁶But Peter made him get up. "Stand up," he said, "I am only a man myself."

²⁷Talking with him, Peter went inside and found a large gathering of people. ²⁸He said to them: "You are well aware that it is against our law for a Jew to associate with a Gentile or visit him. But God has shown me that I should not call any man impure or unclean. ²⁹So when I was sent for, I came without raising any objection. May I ask why you sent for me?"

³⁰Cornelius answered: "Four days ago I was in my house praying at this hour, at three in the afternoon. Suddenly a man in shining clothes stood before me ³¹and said, 'Cornelius, God has heard your prayer and remembered your gifts to the poor. ³²Send to Joppa for Simon who is called Peter. He is a guest in the home of Simon the tanner, who lives by the sea.' ³³So I sent for you immediately, and it was good of you to come. Now we are all here in the presence of God to listen to everything the Lord has commanded you to tell us."

³⁴Then Peter began to speak: "I now realize how true it is that God does not show favoritism ³⁵but accepts men from every nation who fear him and do what is right. ³⁶You know the message God sent to the people of Israel, telling the good news of peace through Jesus Christ, who is Lord of all. ³⁷You know what has happened throughout Judea, beginning in Galilee after the baptism that John preached— ³⁸how God anointed Jesus of Nazareth with the Holy Spirit and power, and how He went around doing good and healing all who were under the power of the devil, because God was with Him.

³⁹"We are witnesses of everything He did in the country of the Jews and in Jerusalem. They killed Him by hanging Him on a tree, ⁴⁰but God raised Him from the dead on the third day and caused Him to be seen. ⁴¹He was not seen by all the people, but by witnesses whom God had already chosen—by us who ate and drank with Him after He rose from the dead. ⁴²He commanded us to preach to the people and to testify that He is the one whom God ap-

pointed as judge of the living and the dead. ⁴³All the prophets testify about Him that everyone who believes in Him receives forgiveness of sins through His name."

⁴⁴While Peter was still speaking these words, the Holy Spirit came on all who heard the message. ⁴⁵The circumcised believers who had come with Peter were astonished that the gift of the Holy Spirit had been poured out even on the Gentiles. ⁴⁶For they heard them speaking in tongues and praising God.

Then Peter said, ⁴⁷"Can anyone keep these people from being baptized with water? They have received the Holy Spirit just as we have." ⁴⁸So he ordered that they be baptized in the name of Jesus Christ. Then they asked Peter to stay with them for a few days.

Acts 10:1-48

Know What It Says

What five or six things do you discover about Cornelius from Acts 10:1-2, 22?

What was a centurion?

What was unusual about Cornelius being a "God-fearing" man?

Considering his job, why would it be unique to be respected by the Jews?

What started Cornelius' learning experience?

Keeping in mind how God began Cornelius' lesson, how does verse 9 suggest God began Peter's lesson?

Understand the Meaning
Describe God's lesson for Peter in your own words.

Why didn't Peter understand? Why did God use a vision to teach him?

What *did* Peter understand?

Who helped Peter find the truth?

In what ways did Peter respond to the lesson even though he didn't totally understand its meaning?

How did Cornelius show he was teachable?

How did Peter show he was teachable?

Scan verses 34-43 to find what lessons Peter learned and what lessons he taught.

What were the results of these two older, experienced, successful, respected men being open to learn from God at this time in their lives? How were they affected by what they learned? Who else was affected by what they learned? (See vv. 23-24)

How It Works in Our Lives

What is one thing you have learned about the knowledge of God's will from this passage?

Now, let's take that principle and understand it in terms of our lives. How is God seeking to teach you this principle?

In what way has He placed a "Cornelius" in your life to cause you to learn something new of His will? Or how has He sent a "Peter" to help you gain new insight?

Are you teachable for what God wants you to learn?

Start Doing It

What would it mean for you to put this principle into practice in your life?

How will you do that? When? With whom?

Can you think of others who will be impacted by your learning this principle? In what way? What could you learn about God by applying this principle in your life?

What one way will you act on what you know from this passage?

GOING THE SECOND MILE

Group Checkup

The Book of Hebrews reminds us, "Let us consider how we may spur one another on toward love and good deeds" (Hebrews 10:24). Of all the members of your group, who is one you can encourage in a specific way to pursue spiritual growth this week?

What would you say to that person regarding your interest in his or her continued growth?

EIGHT

Knowing God in Celebration

GroupSpeak: *"How do I picture God having fun? Well, I think He would fit right into our group fun times. And I think we would all feel most comfortable having Him there. Actually He is there because we are His people having a good time. Maybe His being there among us is what makes it a really good time."*

Celebrate!

Most of us love a good celebration. Parades, fireworks, birthday cakes and candles, victory celebrations over sports events—all these quicken our pulse and bring smiles to our faces. Think of a memorable celebration which you have experienced. What made it exciting and pleasurable to you?

GETTING ACQUAINTED

Planning My Own Party

Which of the following would you choose to include if you could plan your own celebration party?

lots of people	or	a few choice friends ✓
attending an event	or	staying in my home ✓
music ✓	or	entertainment

quiet talking together	or	games and humor
affirming words from friends	or	"roasting" by friends
the element of surprise	or	a meal
doing something you've never done before	or	going back to a memorable place

Who is someone you would like to have around when you celebrate? *NANCY*

Why don't people think of celebrating alone? *You want to share in it w/others*

It seems easy to think of God in hard times—to resort to a higher power and One who is in control. Does it seem just as easy to connect God and celebration in your mind? Why or why not?

If God came to your party, what do you picture Him doing? How do you picture God having a good time?

GAINING INSIGHT

Scripture Study

Charles Schultz made popular the phrase "Happiness is. . . ." Who can forget Linus with his warm blanket and contented countenance! In the midst of coping with pressures and disappointments of life, we all have an image of what happiness is. Though our relationship with God can be sharpened by a distressful situation, God also wants to celebrate our victories and revel in our joyous occasions.

In one of His parables, Jesus gave us a glimpse of what God is like in the midst of a joyous occasion. We see His actions and His expression of joy. While this parable is normally focused on the son, in this session we will focus on the joyous father—a picture of our God in the midst of celebration.

Read a reflection of God having a celebration in the following passage and note characteristics that impress you about this party.

¹¹Jesus continued: "There was a man who had two sons. ¹²The younger one said to his father, 'Father, give me my share of the estate.' So he divided his property between them.

¹³"Not long after that, the younger son got together all he had, set off for a distant country and there squandered his wealth in wild living. ¹⁴After he had spent everything, there was a severe famine in that whole country, and he began to be in need. ¹⁵So he went and hired himself out to a citizen of that country, who sent him to his fields to feed pigs. ¹⁶He longed to fill his stomach with the pods that the pigs were eating, but no one gave him anything.

¹⁷"When he came to his senses, he said, 'How many of my father's hired men have food to spare, and here I am starving to death! ¹⁸I will set out and go back to my father and say to him: Father, I have sinned against heaven and against you. ¹⁹I am no longer worthy to be called your son; make me like one of your hired men.' ²⁰So he got up and went to his father.

"But while he was still a long way off, his father saw him and was filled with compassion for him; he ran to his son, threw his arms around him and kissed him.

²¹"The son said to him, 'Father, I have sinned against heaven and against you. I am no longer worthy to be called your son.'

²²"But the father said to his servants, 'Quick! Bring the best robe and put it on him. Put a ring on his finger and sandals on his feet. ²³Bring the fattened calf and kill it. Let's have a feast and celebrate. ²⁴For this son of mine was dead and is alive again; he was lost and is found.' So they began to celebrate.

²⁵"Meanwhile, the older son was in the field. When he came near the house, he heard music and dancing. ²⁶So

he called one of the servants and asked him what was going on. ²⁷'Your brother has come,' he replied, 'and your father has killed the fattened calf because he has him back safe and sound.'

²⁸"The older brother became angry and refused to go in. So his father went out and pleaded with him. ²⁹But he answered his father, 'Look! All these years I've been slaving for you and never disobeyed your orders. Yet you never gave me even a young goat so I could celebrate with my friends. ³⁰But when this son of yours who has squandered your property with prostitutes comes home, you kill the fattened calf for him!'

³¹" 'My son,' the father said, 'you are always with me, and everything I have is yours. ³²But we had to celebrate and be glad, because this brother of yours was dead and is alive again; he was lost and is found.' "

Luke 15:11-32

What was the setting for this celebration?

Return of a "lost" son

Joy of one coming to know the Lord

What prompted this celebration?

What elements were planned for the party?

Put yourself in the shoes of each of the characters and write a sentence of what you think each would say at this party.

❑ Father: *Praises to God*

❑ Older Son:

❑ Younger Son:

❑ Servant:

Let's focus on the last half of the parable beginning at verse 20.

What were the actions of the father in celebration?

Ran to him, embraced him

What were the father's attitudes in his joy?

Forgiving

What do the father's words tell us about his character?

A compassionate, forgiving, thankful man

What can we learn about God from the good time pictured here?

Which of these findings is particularly significant for you personally? Which have you experienced?

What do we learn about the other characters involved in celebration?

In twos, share in what ways you identify with each character at this party.

God has a way of making good times richer, more fulfilling. When we are grateful and need to express our thanks, He is the fitting recipient for our gratitude and joy. Someone has said, "The worst moment for an atheist is when he is grateful and has no one to thank." God has a way of keeping our joy pure and making it satisfying. He removes the awful feeling of "joy diminished because calamity must be coming." He rejoices in our relationship with Him and shares our joy. What good times do you recall where God was the center for your praise?

GROWING BY DOING

Praise Him

There have been good times in our being together as a group pursuing God. There have been occasions when we have celebrated victories of one another, when we have seen each other grow in knowledge of Him and in likeness to Him. As His people, our natural outlet for sharing our joy with Him is to praise. As you read Psalm 111, listen for the things that give the psalmist joy or become objects of his praise.

¹**Praise the LORD. I will extol the LORD with all my heart in the council of the upright and in the assembly.**

²**Great are the works of the LORD; they are pondered by all who delight in them.**

³**Glorious and majestic are His deeds, and His righteousness endures forever.**

⁴**He has caused His wonders to be remembered; the LORD is gracious and compassionate.**

he provides food for those who fear Him; He remembers His covenan forever.

⁶**He has shown His people the power of His works, giving them the lands of other nations.**

⁷**The words of His hands are faithful and just; all His precepts are trustworthy.**

rock

⁸They are <u>steadfast</u> for ever and ever, done in faithfulness and <u>uprightness.</u> *purity*

⁹He <u>provided redemption</u> for His people; He ordained His covenant forever—holy and awesome is His name.

¹⁰The fear of the LORD is the beginning of wisdom; all who follow His precepts have good understanding. To Him belongs eternal praise.

Psalm 111:1-10

Where does the psalmist say he will praise God?

IN THE BEGINNING

As a part of our celebration, let's do what the psalmist did. Think back over this time in our small group. Let's make a list of significant things that happened in our group—something we learned, answers to prayer, relationships that we've seen develop; specific things that brought joy to us and which we celebrate in praise.

Celebration List

1. *Kennys return – ANSWERED PRAYER*

2. *MaryAnns recovery ANSWERED PRAYER*

3. *FRIENDSHIPS HAVE GROWN*

4.

5.

GOING THE SECOND MILE

Celebrate You

Think of persons in your group who have been important to you, things said that were meaningful to you, actions experienced that cared for you. Now, take a moment to write in the space below a celebration note to a person or to the group expressing your joy over them.

I celebrate you because

Plan to share your celebration note with the object of your celebration.

DEAR SMALL GROUP LEADER:

Picture Yourself As A Leader.

List some words that describe what would excite you or scare you as a leader of your small group.

A Leader Is Not . . .

- ❏ a person with all the answers.
- ❏ responsible for everyone having a good time.
- ❏ someone who does all the talking.
- ❏ likely to do everything perfectly.

A Leader Is . . .

- ❏ someone who encourages and enables group members to discover insights and build relationships.
- ❏ a person who helps others meet their goals, enabling the group to fulfill its purpose.
- ❏ a protector to keep members from being attacked or taken advantage of.
- ❏ the person who structures group time and plans ahead.
- ❏ the facilitator who stimulates relationships and participation by asking questions.
- ❏ an affirmer, encourager, challenger.

❏ enthusiastic about the small group, about God's Word, and about discovering and growing.

What Is Important To Small Group Members?

❏ A leader who cares about them.
❏ Building relationships with other members.
❏ Seeing themselves grow.
❏ Belonging and having a place in the group.
❏ Feeling safe while being challenged.
❏ Having their reasons for joining a group fulfilled.

What Do You Do . . .

If nobody talks—

❏ Wait—show the group members you expect them to answer.
❏ Rephrase a question—give them time to think.
❏ Divide into subgroups so all participate.

If somebody talks too much—

❏ Avoid eye contact with him or her.
❏ Sit beside the person next time. It will be harder for him or her to talk sitting by the leader.
❏ Suggest, "Let's hear from someone else."
❏ Interrupt with, "Great! Anybody else?"

If people don't know the Bible—

❏ Print out the passage in the same translation and hand it out to save time searching for a passage.
❏ Use the same Bible versions and give page numbers.
❏ Ask enablers to sit next to those who may need encouragement in sharing.
❏ Begin using this book to teach them how to study; affirm their efforts.

If you have a difficult individual—

❏ Take control to protect the group, but recognize that exploring differences can be a learning experience.
❏ Sit next to that person.
❏ To avoid getting sidetracked or to protect another group member, you may need to interrupt, saying, "Not all of us feel that way."
❏ Pray for that person before the group meeting.

ONE

Roots

Do you remember the day you met a "Very Important Person"? Do you recall your first encounter with your spouse? Were you in the congregation the day your new pastor came to serve in your church?

The starting point for knowing God is meeting Him and becoming His own. For Israel, that turning point where God established Himself as her God and the Hebrews as His people, was the Exodus. From then on, God began nurturing Israel in His ways and revealing Himself to a people who bore His name. The Exodus became a marker event that would be remembered throughout history. Today, the Christian's journey in knowing God begins with a different marker event—a meaningful relationship with Christ.

Several years ago, Alex Haley produced a best-seller which became a celebration of black "roots" as blacks bonded in their common heritage of African beginnings. As children of God, our common starting point is the Cross. That becomes our "family tree" as we share mutual bonding to Jesus. As we get in touch with our spiritual roots, we identify with the same Savior and realize we are now "family" to one another.

As **Group Leader** of this small group experience, *you* have a choice as to which elements will best fit your group, your style of leadership, and your purposes. After you examine the **Session Objectives,** select the activities under each heading with which to begin your community building. You have many choices.

SESSION OBJECTIVES

√ To get acquainted so we feel at ease in talking about our God.

√ To spend some time showing care for each other as part of the family of God.

√ To reflect on and share encounters which resulted in becoming a child of God.

√ To celebrate our common family tree—the Cross.

√ To clarify group commitments and responsibilities as determined by a group covenant.

GETTING ACQUAINTED   20–25 minutes

If your group is not well acquainted, take time at least to get to know one another's names before beginning this session. If the group is strong in its relational bonds, the following exercises may help to strengthen the group.

Have a group member read aloud **Family Roots.** Then choose one of the following activities to help create a more comfortable, nonthreatening atmosphere for the first meeting of your small group.

Pocket Principle

1 Select an activity according to what you want to accomplish and which will be at a level that will put your group at ease. The size of your group may determine your choice and whether the activity should be adapted to maximize time.

What's in a Family?
Encourage group members to use the questions in this activity to think about their family backgrounds. Ask volunteers to

share some facts about their spiritual heritage, such as the persons responsible for their becoming a part of God's family.

Twins

Ask group members to find someone who shares at least two things in common with them in terms of "roots." After 5–10 minutes, call the group together to share by pairs their common roots.

Optional—Guess Who

Hand out slips of paper and pencils. Ask group members to note on the paper one or two little known facts about their past along with their names. For example: My father was a twin. I moved eight times as a child. I once made sausage on my grandmother's farm in Ohio. Collect the papers and read each one aloud, allowing the group to guess the identity of the writer.

GAINING INSIGHT   30–35 minutes

Pocket Principle

2 Participation is key if the group is to become more than the leader's group. If you want people to get involved in applying truth in their lives, allow them to be involved in discovering truth for themselves. Expect them to think and share, not be spoon-fed. Ask questions.

Marker Events

Birthdays are significant to our humanity. Our spiritual origins are key "roots" in our spiritual development. Discuss the following questions:

❑ **What marker events in our nation's history are still remembered today with celebrations?** (the birth of our nation—July 4, Armistice Day, Washington's and Lincoln's birthdays).

❑ **What marker events would you list in Israel's history?** (the giving of the 10 Commandments, the Exodus, the Exile)

Have group members take the **Exodus Quiz.** Then check your answers.

Point out that God wanted Israel to remember her spiritual roots of the Passover and the Exodus. Encourage the group to look for specific things that would jog ·the Hebrews' memories as they read Exodus 12:14-17, 21-22, 25-27; 13:11-14; 15:1-13.

Pocket Principle

3 For maximum insight when reading Scripture, (1) ask all group members to look at the passage; (2) give them something specific to look or listen for; (3) select someone who reads well to do the reading; (4) limit the number of verses to the fewest possible (summarize a section which need not be read).

Explain that the methods God suggested in these passages included:

❏ Setting aside a "spiritual holiday"

❏ Meeting together to recall what God has done

❏ Eating a special meal

❏ Talking about their salvation with the next generation

❏ Special "setting apart" of the firstborn to remind them of the price of redemption

❏ Singing a special song declaring what God has done

After reading 1 Corinthians 11:23-26, discuss how God wants us to recall on a regular basis Jesus' sacrifice on Calvary. Ask volunteers to share how they met Jesus. You may want to record on a calendar each person's spiritual birthday so the group can celebrate it. For those who can't remember the exact date—pick a spot on the calendar for their day of remembrance. If you have non-Christians present, you may prefer to ask several chosen group members to share how they met Jesus.

94

GROWING BY DOING   15–20 minutes

Celebrate!
Share with your group the following ideas for remembering what God has done:

☐ We can set aside our own "memorial days" to praise and remember what God has done for us.

☐ Take time to remember each person's spiritual birthday.

☐ Set apart our "firsts" as an offering to God, e.g., the first part of our paycheck, the first day of the week, the first hour of the day, the first day of vacation, the first day of the month, our first-born, etc. as a way of remembering what God has done.

Song of Deliverance
Use Exodus 15 as a model for composing a song that incorporates specifics from your group's sharing of their salvation histories. Exodus 15 will give them ideas of expressions to use.

Optional—Enjoying Our Inheritance
Hand out "inheritance" slips which contain verses describing something that is ours because of our salvation. As a group, read the verses and identify the spiritual inheritance found in each passage. Then, share a time of thanks with group members, mentioning in their thanksgiving to God what their verses suggest is ours because of salvation.

Scripture	Spiritual Inheritance
John 10:23	security
Romans 5:1-2	peace, grace
Romans 5:9	saved from wrath
Romans 6:8	eternal life
Romans 8:14	led by Spirit
Romans 8:1	no condemnation
Romans 8:21	free
Romans 8:26	prayed for by Spirit
Romans 8:38-39	love of God
Ephesians 2:18	good works
Ephesians 3:12	hope
1 Peter 2:9-10	light

95

Optional—Worship Ideas

To introduce the theme of joy and delight in God who gives us salvation, read Isaiah 61:10 and Revelation 19:6-8. Songs of worship should be those where all are familiar with the words. These might include "Blessing, Glory and Honor," "Amazing Grace," "Now I Belong to Jesus," "Redeemed, How I Love to Proclaim It," "To God Be the Glory," "God Forgave My Sin," "Jesus, Name Above All Names," "No Other Plea," "And Can It Be."

A fitting way to close is by singing "Happy Birthday" to all, each inserting the name of a person in the group as you rejoice over each person's birth into the family of God. You may want to close with cake and candles to celebrate this event.

GOING THE SECOND MILE   5 minutes

Group Checkup

Challenge the group to spend some time during the next few days thinking about ways to keep the memories of their spiritual roots alive. They can complete this section on their own. However, encourage them to pray for each other.

GROWING AS A LEADER

Personal Assessment

To feel that what we have done is worthwhile, we need to see that we have changed or grown as a result of time and energy. A thoughtful appraisal with or without a colleague's feedback is the first step in moving forward in growth. You can teach yourself practical small group skills. Sharing these insights about yourself with another person is a sure way to grow.

TWO

Knowing God

The relationships we value shape our lives. Think of two or three primary relationships in your life at the present time. How would your life be different were those relationships absent? The most important relationship possible is that of knowing God—personally and intimately as One who knows us more completely than any other.

Martyred missionary Jim Elliot, as a collegian, wrote, "Lord, let my life be an example of the value of knowing God." His life, though shortened by an Auca Indian spear, still speaks to generations today of the worth of his supreme commitment.

In this session we will be examining what it means to know God. As **Group Leader** of this small group experience, *you* have a choice as to which elements will best fit your group, your style of leadership, and your purposes. After you examine the **Session Objectives**, select the activities under each heading with which to begin your community building. You have many choices.

SESSION OBJECTIVES

✓ To realize what it means to know God—not just know about God.

✓ To see situations in our lives as opportunities to know God better.

✓ To leave with a desire to know God in a more intimate way.

✓ To rejoice over the privilege of knowing God and initiate steps toward getting to know Him better.

GETTING ACQUAINTED   20–25 minutes

Have a group member read aloud **It's Who You Know.** Then choose one of the following activities to help create a more comfortable, nonthreatening atmosphere.

Pocket Principle

1 **To save time and avoid confusion, always hand out or display questions you want dealt with in groups. Stating a question in two different ways often helps people grasp meaning.**

Letter of Recommendation
Have the group fill in their letters of recommendation for God. Then ask volunteers to share their reference letters.

Optional—Knowing Yourself and God
Have group members complete this sentence with something that reveals who they are: I am a person who. . . . Now, have them complete this sentence with something that reveals who they think God is: My God is. . . .

GAINING INSIGHT   30–35 minutes

Let Me Introduce You To . . .
Divide into three teams and assign each a section (titles, actions, words) to each team. Instruct each team to investi-

gate and come up with information about God and who He is. After 10 minutes, gather together and have each team briefly share its findings.

Optional—Ten Most Important Things about God
Compile a group list of the 10 most important things they know about God. The best procedure is to brainstorm, listing items on a large sheet. Then decide on the 10 most vital.

Scripture Study
After a group member reads aloud Exodus 3:9-15, discuss the following questions.

❑ **What was Moses' first concern? How would you phrase Moses' question in your own words?** (God, You don't know me—I can't do it.)

❑ **How did God respond to Moses' question?** (He didn't tell Moses how great He was or affirm Moses' outstanding strengths. Instead, He promised His presence and sign of approval.)

❑ **What was Moses' second question to God? Had Israel really forgotten who God was—His dealings with Abraham, Isaac, and Jacob? Did they just not know what to call Him?** (No, Israel knew about God's encounters with their fathers. Moses was asking for something more. To the Hebrews, the word *name* meant more than just an identifying title. A name represented and expressed the character and personality of the one who bore it. To know a person's name was to have a relationship with him or her. This was especially true of the name of God. In asking for His name, the people desired to learn what God's relationship was to them. He had been the "God of the fathers"—who was He now?)

❑ **What three things did God reveal about Himself in verses 14-15?** (In responding to Moses' request, God first revealed that He wants to be known. When God answered, "I am Who I am," He was not using double-talk to conceal His identity. This was a Hebrew form of defining something in terms of itself. By using this form, God was ex-

99

pressing overwhelming definiteness or intensity. It can be translated "indeed." The same meaning is seen in God's statement, "I will be gracious to whom I will be gracious." The Hebrews understood this form to mean, "I am indeed gracious." God was also letting Moses know who He is. His answer is actually, "I am indeed He who is here—ready to help and to act." God indicated that He has opened to us His very being and has given us access to Himself. Finally, God revealed that He wants to be remembered forever by this very name. He always is known as the One who is there for us—who is open to know and act for us.)

Ask a group member to read Exodus 33:12-14. Then discuss these questions.

❏ **What was God's response to Moses' request?** (God responded by promising His presence so Moses could come to know Him.)

❏ **How does God's "Presence" in a situation allow us to know Him?** (As God speaks and acts in our midst, we can observe His character and patterns of operation which reflect who He is. His presence would reveal His will in guidance and give us a sense of His strength.)

Ask volunteers to share their responses to the remaining questions.

GROWING BY DOING   15–20 minutes

History with God
Divide into small groups and share times when God has revealed Himself through situations in your lives. After a short time of sharing, reassemble the group and compile a list of specific ways that knowing God has affected the lives of persons in your group. Ask: **How has knowing God affected your lifestyle? Your relationships? Your outlook on life? Your plans? Your attitude and perspective? Your schedule? Your values?**

Pocket Principle

2 Evaluate: Is it important that every person share and thus have ownership in the group? Or do we need a sense of unity and togetherness by inviting a few to share in the hearing of all? Adapt your "doing" to small units or as one large unit so group members grow in the dimension they need.

Optional—Worship Ideas
Choose worship music that expresses the theme of relating to God. Possibilities include: "The Greatest Thing in All My Life Is Knowing You," "I Love You, Lord," "My Jesus, I Love You," "What a Friend We Have in Jesus," "Be Still and Know That I Am God," "Open Our Eyes, Lord."

Set apart one another with prayers of dedication to the supreme purpose of living to know God—not just to serve Him or to do His will—but to embrace the primary purpose for which He saved us.

GOING THE SECOND MILE   5 minutes

A Changed Life
Challenge the group to complete this section on their own. Encourage them to read the Scriptures and consider what each one tells them about God. They should put a √ by any of the statements which closely reflect their thoughts or feelings.

Optional—Planning to Know God Better
If time permits, you may want to take time to share with one another specific desires and ways you plan to get to know God. Ask each group member to select one statement in this section to complete. Divide into pairs and ask each pair to share their responses to the statements and covenant to pray for each other during the next month.

THREE

Being Known

A magazine ad describes a device which can be inserted into the ear which will allow the overhearing of conversations up to 50 feet away. The ad includes a word of caution—"Do not use this device without obtaining permission from the conversationalists." This and other scientific bugging devices cause an uneasiness in the hearts of most of us as we fear our privacy being invaded.

Psychologists tell us that we resist self-disclosure because being known has implications which seem negative to the individual. We resist self-knowledge because when we know our inadequacies and inner motives, we face responsibility and perhaps the need to change. Some people hesitate to self-disclose because they fear the intimacy disclosure could breed with another and they don't want another to be that close. The "reverse halo" effect also prompts us to be concealing. Just as a person who is recognized as superior in one area is often given the "halo" of being superior in all areas of life, so the person who reveals weakness or inadequacy may be credited with doubtful worth in other realms of being.

In contrast to this fear of being known is the security that comes with being known and accepted. There is a resonance in the heart that hears from another: "I know, I understand because I know, I accept because I know." Self-disclosure can lead to greater love. When we love, we want to know more of who the person is. The sharing of the self can increase the intimate caring within a relationship. As we focus on God as the Knower and ourselves as the ones known to the deepest depths of our being, the goal is that we might respond with an intense pursuit of knowing God in greater depth.

As **Group Leader** of this small group experience, *you* have a choice as to which elements will best fit your group, your style of leadership, and your purposes. After you examine the **Session Objectives,** select the activities under each heading with which to begin your community building. You have many choices.

SESSION OBJECTIVES

√ To realize what it means to be known by God.
√ To feel comfortable and affirmed in being known by God.
√ To respond to the awareness that God knows us by wanting to know God in greater depth.

GETTING ACQUAINTED   20–25 minutes

Have a group member read aloud **The Fear of Being Known.** Then choose one of the following activities to help create a more comfortable, nonthreatening atmosphere.

How Well Do You Know Me?
Have group members find a partner and without discussion, put a √ by the answer they feel their partner would select for each of the questions.

Share answers together and discuss areas where there was definite awareness of how the other person would respond. Have the group talk about how they "knew" the right answer by something they have observed in that person.

Best Friend
Ask each group member to think of one person outside this group who knows him/her better than anyone else. Ask vol-

unteers to stand behind an empty chair and introduce themselves as they would expect their "best friend" to do it.

Optional — Fact or Fiction
There is a common expression that says, "To know me is to love me." Discuss the meaning or implication of this statement. Ask: **Do you think this statement is true? How have you found it to be true or untrue in your experience?**

Optional — Three Questions
Ask: **If you could ask only three questions in order to get to know a person — which three questions would you ask that will give you the most information?** After the group has decided on the three most profitable questions, have group members try them out on each other.

GAINING INSIGHT   30–35 minutes
Pocket Principle

1 Avoid long monologues in small group learning times. Choose material which is relevant. Ask rhetorical questions to keep people involved. Add your own illustrations and invite others to respond with theirs. Help members participate, even if only nodding to questions which each answers personally.

If You Really Knew Me
As you and your group work through this section, share the following story from Bruce Larson's *Thirty Days To A New You* (Zondervan, 1974).

Most of us can identify with Bruce Larson's account of the soldier in the Fort Benning, Georgia infantry training camp who encountered grits for the first time. That first morning in the infantry the newly recruited seventeen-year-old sat down to breakfast with 10 other men at a family-style table. He noted that in the center of that table was a large bowl of something that looked like *Cream of Wheat*. Scooping up a large amount in his bowl, he poured milk and sugar on top.

Across the table a tall mountain boy stared at him bug-eyed. In amazement he asked the new recruit from the north, "Is that the way you eat grits?"

Immediately, the seventeen-year-old who had heard of grits but had never seen them before realized his mistake and mentally filed away this new information away for future reference. But rather than declare his ignorance, he smiled confidently and asserted, "Sure. This is how we eat grits in Chicago." The questioner across the table watched in amazement the Northerner's consumption of the terrible tasting concoction while he ate his grits the proper way with butter and salt.

Several mornings later the new recruit found himself sitting at the breakfast table with the same rangy mountaineer. Grits were served again, and under his watchful eye the Chicago kid obediently scooped up some grits, and poured on milk and sugar. Rather than admit his error he choked down the sweet, sticky mess.

This desire to hide because we are afraid what will happen when someone discovers the real us isn't new. Most of us identify with Adam and Eve who hid when they heard the Lord God walking in the garden (Genesis 3:8-10). Many a child has hidden the stolen cookie with the approach of parental footsteps. Many an adult has hidden behind the proverbial "busyness" when the accountable person approaches for an answer.

Statements like "I would never have thought that about you," upon revealing a bit of the real you, reinforce our fear of being judged and condemned. In John Powell's little book, *Why Am I Afraid To Tell You Who I Am?* (Tabor, 1969), he answers, "I am afraid because, if I tell you who I am, you may not like who I am, and that is all that I have."

Scripture Study
Explain that Scripture assures us that God loves us and that God knows us. Help your group catch a glimpse of God's kind of knowledge by reading aloud Psalm 139:1-6, 13-16. Point out how personally the psalmist describes the knowledge of God. Then discuss the following questions.

❑ **In verse 1, what does the word *search* suggest?** (The Hebrew word for *search* used here means "to dig." God has dug below the surface and knows the real person. As customs agents search goods entering the country, as detectives search for clues—God "digs" into who we are.)

❑ **What do the first set of contrasts in verse 2 (sit and rise) indicate about God's knowledge?** (God knows our quiet times and our active times. How many times have we sat down today? Stood up? Translate this into specifics: "Today God knew me when I sat down to.... He knew why I did that at that time. He knew what I was doing.")

❑ **What do you picture God observing in you today?** (He knows our most common and casual acts as well as the most important ones of our day.)

❑ **What realm of God's knowledge is highlighted in the second half of verse 2? How many of our personal relationships would change if people knew what we were really thinking? What changes would it make in business deals? In teaching and preaching? In parenting?** (Not just our acts, but our thoughts are known to God. He knows our subconscious, how and what we think about. Comic strips often capture a person's thoughts in a cloud overhead so the reader gets the gist of the content. It is a relief not to have that kind of visible cloud revealing our thoughts in real life.)

❑ **What sphere of living does verse 3 accentuate?** (God knows our going out, our lying down, our running and resting. The verb used here is translated *discern*, or in some translations, *scrutinize*. It literally means "to sift"—to go through a sieve as with flour. God is intimately acquainted with all our ways. He knows our patterns and habits. He knows whether we button our shirts up or down, whether we put catsup on eggs, whether we step into our right shoes first.)

❑ **What does God know according to verse 4?** (God knows our words before they come off our tongues. If only we could know this, perhaps we wouldn't say what we say.

106

As a child put it, "How do I know what I think, until I hear what I have to say?" Our words house our thoughts.)

❏ **In verse 5 the psalmist expresses feelings that accompany the insights he is sharing. How would you identify the feeling he is conveying with his words?** (We are encircled by God and His knowledge of us. He knows all our past and He foreknows all our future.)

❏ **According to verse 13, what does God know about our past?** (He knew and formed us in embryo stage.)

❏ **Based on verse 15, what does He know about my bone and muscle structure?** (Our frame, or bone and muscle structure, was designed by God. He knew and designed our height, athletic ability, way we walk, etc.)

❏ **What are the words used for God's action on our unborn substance?** (*created* or *made, knit together, woven together*. The last of these three is a Hebrew word symbolizing "embroidered.")

❏ **Finally, what does verse 16 indicate about God's knowledge of us?** (He knows not only the number of days allotted to our lives, but everything that those days contain. We are fascinated with the resources of the human mind. People under hypnosis have been able to recall such trivial details as the wallpaper pattern in the room where they celebrated their fifth birthday, as well as each birthday gift received. God not only knows past birthday parties, but all the plans for our future ones. He knows our days and minutes.

GROWING BY DOING   15–20 minutes

Knowing God Knows Me
After a group member reads Psalm 139:23-24, discuss these questions.

❏ **How would you describe the psalmist's response to God's knowledge of him?** (Knowing that God had such complete knowledge brought surrender—a feeling of trust.)

❑ **What does he open up to God for investigation in these verses?** (His heart, thoughts, actions, and submission to be led.)

Invite each group member to write God a brief prayer that expresses their response to the fact that God knows them.

GOING THE SECOND MILE 5 minutes

Reflect

Challenge group members to take time each evening to reflect back over their day with God.

FOUR

Knowing God in Hard Times

"Fair-weather friends" is a phrase used to describe people who can't be found when times become difficult and there is a cost to be paid. Such a label depicts lack of depth, self-centeredness, and a fickleness that cannot withstand pressure and pain. None of us longs for "foul weather" to hit our lives but when it does, it's comforting to have relationships that weather hard and difficult times.

It is a fact of life that we often come to know God more intimately during the rough times of life than we do when things are going smoothly. When no one else can grasp the depth of pain or pressure, we feel that God alone understands. In fact it is often in those moments that we come to know God and place faith in Him to a higher degree than we ever thought possible.

The emphasis in this session will be on what we can discover of God when life becomes difficult to cope with. As **Group Leader** of this small group experience, *you* have a choice as to which elements will best fit your group, your style of leadership, and your purposes. Because of the depth of sharing desired in this session, you will want to do everything possible to make this a safe, secure atmosphere in which to share meaningfully. After you examine the **Session Objectives**, select the activities under each heading with which to begin your community building. You have many choices.

SESSION OBJECTIVES

√ To become aware of how hard times often lead us to know God.

√ To share experiences and become a part of each other's lives.

√ To be supportive of one another in present difficult situations.

GETTING ACQUAINTED   20–25 minutes

Have a group member read aloud **A Little Rain Must Fall.** Then choose one of the following activities to help create a more comfortable, nonthreatening atmosphere.

Pocket Principle

1 Security in a group is often determined by the process used to share. Build safety by preparing group members ahead of time with clear purposes and specific directions for what you are going to do. The more understanding a person has, the greater the feeling of security. Modeling (the leader sharing first) is an observable boundary which helps group members grasp what is expected. Sharing in twos or fours is safer than with the whole group. Finally, giving a person some indication that he or she has been heard (a nod, affirmation, rephrasing, acknowledgment of the emotional feeling tied in with the facts shared) helps him or her know that his or her precious contribution is received, regarded, and kept safe by another.

Your Difficult Times

Have group members think about some stressful situations they have experienced and what they have learned from those difficult times.

110

True, False, or Maybe

Instruct group members to respond to each statement by writing True, False, or Maybe. Then discuss which of the statements most group members feel comfortable with. Ask: **What other questions about difficult circumstances do you have?**

Optional—Hard Time Barometer

Explain that most times we are given no choice in the hard experiences that come to us in life. And usually everyone fears one kind more than another: "I just don't think I could go through. . . ." "The thing I would have the hardest time coping with is. . . ." Ask group members to share in twos what type of "hard experience" they fear most and why.

Optional—Responding to Loss

Ask: **How have you observed that people handle difficult experiences and suffering?** Suggest the following responses.

❑ become hardened
❑ feel guilt and introspection
❑ blame others/circumstances
❑ feel they are being punished/disciplined
❑ soften/become moldable
❑ feel anger/resentment—why me?

Ask: **What do you think is at the heart of their responding the way they do?**

Pocket Principle

2 Feelings are a necessary part of a group. In fact, feelings may be the most accurate indicators of who we really are. Beware of using feeling stoppers which tell a person that feelings aren't OK. Four common feeling stoppers are: Denial ("You don't really feel that way."); Cheering ("You won't feel that way forever."); Reasoning ("You don't have to feel that way because God says . . ."); Shaming ("I'm surprised at you. You know better."). Feelings are not right or wrong—we do not have control over them. We do have control over what we do with them. But they must be received first. Once heard, then they can be worked through.

GAINING INSIGHT   30–35 minutes

Purpose and Gain
Ask group members to take turns reading aloud this section.

Optional—"So That's"
Let's look at the "so that's" which give value to some difficult situations noted in Scripture. Have group members read the following passages and determine the purpose for each difficult situation.

❑ John 9:1-3—The man was born blind so that . . .

❑ John 11:14-15—Lazarus' sickness ended in death so that . . .

❑ Romans 8:17-18—We must share suffering with Christ so that . . .

❑ 2 Corinthians 1:3-6—Another reason we must experience suffering is so that . . .

❑ 2 Corinthians 12:7, 9-10—Paul had to experience his thorn in the flesh so that . . .

❑ Philippians 1:12-14—Paul suffered imprisonment so that . . .

Scripture Study
Ask a group member to read Romans 8:26-29, 31, 33, 37-39. Then discuss the following questions.

❑ Notice how verse 28 begins with three powerful words—"And we know." To get the full impact of the word know, let's substitute some words. For instance, the verse doesn't begin with "And we wish."

What else does it not say? (hope, suppose, think, desire, trust)

❑ **What happens when we face life's experiences with this kind of confident knowledge?** (Video tapes allow us the luxury of replaying experiences that have already happened. When you know how the game ends, you look at individual setbacks and enemy gains in a different light. When you know you're a winner, temporary setbacks look different.)

❑ **This confident kind of knowledge contrasts sharply to what the author has just written in verse 26. What do we not know in the midst of our weakened condition?** (How to pray. In the midst of a difficult situation, there are times when we feel very weak in the arena of prayer. At that point we know not how to pray the way we should.)

❑ **Why do you think we feel this inadequacy and confusion?** (Emotional stress can rob us of rationality and limit our awareness of alternatives. We can become paralyzed in looking at things from one perspective only, and it is difficult to be objective.)

❑ **When we realize that we are in this state of helplessness and are seemingly unable to pray effectively, what encouragements does verse 28 provide? In what ways does knowing that "God works" give us courage to go on?** (We know He can take charge. Even though we don't know what to ask for, we are assured He is in control.)

❑ **How do the last four words of verse 28 give direction to His "working"?** (He has a purpose. He is not just trying to put together random pieces of life as they happen to us—and then has to regroup as best He can. Our lives and our circumstances are His project from start to finish.)

❑ **What kinds of feelings are cultivated in you when you realize that God's knowledge and perspective is far beyond your own?** (A sense of peace that One more knowledgeable is in control. A sense of hope and expectation that there are alternatives and answers available which, though hidden from us, are options for God. A feeling of satisfaction that there is order and accomplishment in what God does. A sense of joy that good is being achieved.)

❑ **According to verse 29, what is one of those "good" results that God purposes?** (To be conformed means "to bring to the same form." Our destiny is to become like Him. In obedience to that likeness there will be the experience of difficulties as our character is forged.)

❑ **What benefits of that confidence did Paul declare in verses 33-35?** (No one can bring valid charges against us. Knowing we are loved enables us to see circumstances from a different perspective, and none of them can wall us off from the love of Christ. There is no difficult situation which can come between us and the love of Christ.)

After group members list their own possibilities for difficult circumstances paralleling those Paul lists, read aloud the question found in Romans 8:35. Then have group members note their own extenuating circumstances. For example: **"Who shall separate us from the love of Christ?" Shall financial collapse? Loss of relationship with a spouse through divorce? Being unjustly treated for doing right?** Conclude by reading verses 37-39 in unison.

 ## GROWING BY DOING   15–20 minutes

Questions for Reflection
Divide the group into twos or fours. Ask each small group to share together their responses to the questions in this section. Have each group read in unison Romans 8:28 and close in prayer.

Optional—Worship Ideas
Celebrate the greatness of God by reading God's response to Job when Job questioned God's fairness in the circumstances He allowed. Pick portions of Job 38 which reveal the unanswerable questions God put to Job. End with Job 42:1-2

where Job acquiesces to God's authority and power to do what He wants with the creatures He has made.

Include hymns that reflect the greatness of God such as "How Great Thou Art," "He Is Able," "Great Is Thy Faithfulness," "Great Is the Lord," "God Is My Refuge," "Jehovah-Jireh," or "Thou Art a Shield for Me."

You may want to use the responsive phrase, "God is greater," after each statement of a situation faced by someone in your small group. For example, "Our world is filled with injustice from the government of South Africa to the streets of the ghetto. But God is greater than injustice."

GOING THE SECOND MILE   5 minutes

Group Checkup
Challenge group members to complete this section on their own.

GROWING AS A LEADER

Personal Assessment
Take time to think through these questions as you evaluate this session.

❑ What indicated to you that group members felt safe or felt insecure during this session?

❑ Can you pinpoint anything you did that fostered security?

❑ What did you learn about helping persons self-disclose that will enable you to be more pastoral in succeeding sessions?

❑ How was pastoral care evident during this sensitive session? Were there persons who demonstrated they may have this as a gift? How can you encourage them to exercise this gift in your midst?

115

FIVE

Knowing God Through His Will

As humans we all long for inside information on what is going to happen in the future. Some years ago a popular television program was called "You Are There." This program was built on the awful dilemma of knowing what was going to happen to the participants while they were oblivious to the momentous events that were about to take place. Thus persons merrily boarded the *Titanic* unaware of the impending disaster. But the viewer knew and felt the weight of helplessness to change the course of events.

We long to know the future because we want to avoid the bad and experience the good. Nancy Reagan made headlines after word leaked out that she had asked an astrologer to chart her husband's schedule after he narrowly missed being killed. Even the dinner guest who casually breaks open a fortune cookie is expressing desire to know the future.

This session's focus is on the Christian's desire to mesh with the plans of God—to choose God's way without knowing the future implications. As **Group Leader** of this small group experience, *you* have a choice as to which elements will best fit your group, your style of leadership, and your purposes. After you examine the **Session Objectives**, select the activities under each heading with which to begin your community building. You have many choices.

116

SESSION OBJECTIVES

√ To realize how knowing God relates to knowing His will.

√ To know God and His principles as a basis for doing His will.

√ To focus on one area in which to practice doing His will.

GETTING ACQUAINTED   20–25 minutes

Have a group member read aloud **Cutting Through the Misconceptions.** Then choose one of the following activities to help create a more comfortable, nonthreatening atmosphere.

Hungry for the Future

Ask group members to brainstorm ways that people seek to know the future. Be sure to mention these methods: horoscopes, astrology, parapsychology, ESP, counseling, psychology, intuition, feelings, signs, open/closed doors.

Agree/Disagree

Divide into small groups to share comments provoked by responding to the Agree/Disagree statements.

Optional—Personal History Interview

Choose two or three persons who have been contacted ahead of time to respond to this request: **Share an experience where you have known the guidance of God, where you knew what God's will was even as you were doing it.**

Optional—Panel

Select 3–4 people to serve as a panel and supply each person with a card on which is written TRUE on one side and FALSE on the other side. After you read the following statements often made about God's will, each panelist votes as to whether he or she feels the statement is valid. After voting is complete, invite each panelist to comment on his or her response.

- ❏ Putting out a "fleece" is a good way to find God's will.
- ❏ Only one choice in several options is God's will.
- ❏ There is no second chance if you make a "wrong choice." If you miss God's will, you have to live with it.
- ❏ God's will is specific, not general.
- ❏ Living a godly life ensures you will know the will of God.
- ❏ Opening the Bible and reading the first verse you see is a way of finding out God's will.
- ❏ If it's God's will, it will fall into place without hurdles—no closed doors.
- ❏ You can't trust your feelings—they will probably be the opposite of God's will.
- ❏ If it's God's will, it will probably be hard to accept, something you wouldn't naturally choose.
- ❏ God's will primarily involves the major decisions of life, not common everyday events.

Pocket Principle

1 **What can you do if a group member gives an obvious wrong answer? Ask: "What causes you to say that?" "Where do you see that in God's Word?" "What do the rest of you think about that?" Or take the blame for miscommunication, "Perhaps I didn't ask that in the right way."**

GAINING INSIGHT   30–35 minutes

Finding God's Will

As you and your group work through this section, discuss what view of God is reflected by each of these statements.

- ❏ **We should put out a "fleece" to find God's will.** (This statement refers to Gideon's response when God made plain to Gideon that he was to deliver Israel from Midian. He knew God's will—he wouldn't accept it, so he asked for a sign. See Judges 6:12ff. It happened only once as God endured Gideon's questioning. It was not to discover the will of God but to bolster Gideon's faith. It implies that God doesn't mean what He says—that we need a supernatural event to prove He means His commands.)

❑ **If we miss the will of God, we must live with second best.** (This view suggests that God is helpless and dependent on our choice. He is powerless to accomplish what He desires in any other way but one.)

❑ **If we ask for God's will, He will probably send us to Africa, make us stay single, ask us to give up our new car, etc.** (This view suggests that God is a killjoy.)

❑ **If it is God's will, it will fall in place and everything will go smoothly.** (This view suggests that God, if He is good, doesn't allow hardships, difficulties, suffering.)

Pocket Principle

1 Using many different Scripture passages can have a negative, overwhelming effect. To ensure maximum value, make sure everyone is looking at each passage as it is discussed. Give group members something to look for. Clearly identify what is being asked and allow time for participants to find answers.

Now have group members work through the four principles regarding God's will and then talk about some areas where we focus on it in our lives.

Principle #1
Knowing God Is Key to Knowing His Will

Have a group member read John 10:24-27, 37-38. Then discuss these questions.

❑ **What did the Jews want to know?** (If Jesus was the Messiah.)

❑ **What was Jesus' response to their request?** (That He had already told them through words and acts, but they didn't hear because they wouldn't believe.)

❑ **What does He suggest as the reason why God's will was hidden from them?** (They didn't belong to Him, and thus didn't listen or respond.)

❑ **What was the purpose of the wonders He performed?** (To reveal who He was.)

119

❑ **Why do you think it was difficult for the Jews to see the truth the miracles were attempting to portray?** (They didn't want to see it because it conflicted with what they already believed. They had achieved status and accomplishment in their present system so any change would threaten them.)

After a group member reads John 9:1-16, 24-34, discuss the following questions.

❑ **In verse 16, we see that the religious leaders revealed their limited understanding of who Jesus was. What kept them from believing and perceiving truth?** (The Pharisees continued to hunt for the truth by asking the formerly blind man who Jesus was. But their unbelief would not permit them to see the truth. They even questioned the man's parents.)

❑ **When they questioned the formerly blind man a second time, what conclusions did they come to?** (They concluded that Jesus was a sinner. They also concluded that the man was a disciple of One who had no authority whereas they claimed Moses as authority and credible mentor. They assumed that because the man was born a sinner (and thus suffered blindness) he didn't have any right to "inform" them.

❑ **How does this incident in John 9 illustrate what Jesus declared in John 10:25-26?** (They were oblivious to what the miracle declared about Jesus.)

Principle #2
It Is God's Nature to Reveal Himself and His Will
Have your group members read John 14:8-11. Then discuss what evidence you find that God wants us to know Him.

Principle #3
Knowing God's Principles Helps Us Know God's Will
Explain that the implication regarding God's will in Hebrews 13:21 is that we can have everything we need for doing His will. Ask several group members to read: John 5:19, 30; John 8:28-29; John 12:49. Then discuss how Jesus knew what to do to accomplish God's will. Note that Jesus knew the principles on which God operated because He observed or heard them from the Father.

Principle #4
Application of God's Principles Will Lead Us into Doing God's Will
Help your group form some guidelines for doing the will of God by examining the following passages and sharing what these verses tell us about doing God's will.

❏ **John 7:17**—Being willing to do the will of God gives us insight into truth.

❏ **Jeremiah 29:11**—That willingness to become whatever God wills is based on what we know of God—that He is good and that His plans are good.

❏ **Romans 12:1-2**—By living lives that are obedient to God and by allowing His Word to give us new perspectives and insights, our minds/attitudes are made new. This gives us a grasp on evaluating and choosing what God's will is. J.B. Phillips paraphrases Romans 12:2 as follows: "Don't let the world around you squeeze you into its own mold, but let God re-make you so that your whole attitude of mind is changed. Thus you will prove in practice that the will of God is good, acceptable to Him and perfect."

❏ **Ephesians 5:8-10**—Living in obedience helps us discover what pleases God.

❏ **1 John 5:14**—Praying according to the principles of His will means our prayers will be answered. Knowing God allows us to trust God. In trusting God and doing what He says, we then prove that His will is GOOD.

Review the four main principles before moving on.

 GROWING BY DOING   15–20 minutes

God's Will Now
Divide group members into threes or fours to share which of the above guidelines affect our lives in doing the will of God. Ask the small groups to share responses to the questions in this section.

GOING THE SECOND MILE 5 minutes

A Person After God's Own Heart
Challenge group members to read 1 Samuel 17:32-47 on their
own to see how David knew and acted on the will of God.

GROWING AS A LEADER

Personal Assessment
As you evaluate this session, consider the following questions.

How did you handle differences of opinion in this session?

Were there any evident wrong answers given? How did you
respond?

In what ways did you help group members go deeper in their
thinking?

Was everyone involved in the sharing? If not, why not?

Since there were many choices of learning activities in this
session, why did you select the ones you did? What principles
did you practice in determining your selection?

What is one leadership function you saw yourself doing well
in this session?

How would your group members suggest you grow?

Who is a person you could begin equipping for future leadership in your group?

SIX

Knowing God Through the Sacraments

We are surrounded with symbols that convey meaning and messages to our minds. What do the following symbols represent in our culture?

- ❑ Saluting?
- ❑ The lighting of candles on a cake?
- ❑ Fireworks?
- ❑ Receiving a dozen red roses?
- ❑ Finding a skull and crossbones on a bottle?

The Christian church is rich in symbols that express meaning to knowledgeable believers. The divided chancel, the central pulpit, the three-faceted trefoil, the fish, the dove, even the church spire—all are meant to speak messages about what we believe.

God has called us to be diligent to observe two significant events which reflect special messages to those who participate—Baptism and Communion. Each of these events is a symbol of our relationship to God and to the body of Christ.

As **Group Leader** of this small group experience, *you* have a choice as to which elements will best fit your group, your style of leadership, and your purposes. After you examine the **Session Objectives**, select the activities under each heading with which to begin your community building. You have many choices.

SESSION OBJECTIVES

√ To know God in a new way through the experience of sharing a common heritage of Baptism and Communion.
√ To prepare to participate meaningfully in celebration.
√ To understand the significance of what we do in this experience.
√ To experience being bound together in a shared community of worship and love.

GETTING ACQUAINTED   20–25 minutes

Have a group member read aloud **A Common Heritage.** Then choose one of the following activities to help create a more comfortable, nonthreatening atmosphere.

Pocket Principle

1 It is important to select a getting acquainted activity in which all can participate. Choose wisely according to the experience and knowledge level of your group members. Adapt exercises or team up those who are more biblically literate with newer believers.

Test Yourself
Have group members work together to test their knowledge of the sacraments. Answers are found in Matthew 26:26-29; Mark 14:22-25; Luke 22:14-20; 1 Corinthians 10:16-17ff (KJV and NASB); Mark 1:9; 1 Corinthians 11:23-30; John 4:2.

Optional — A Memorable Sacrament
Ask group members to share when they were baptized or experienced a memorable Communion. Ask: **What made this particular event meaningful?**

124

Optional—Identify These Symbols
Give each group member a paper on which is sketched a visual symbol. Give each person the opportunity to share with the group what his or her symbol represents. Visual symbols might include: a dove, a fish, oil, a veil, fire, scepter, lamb, overflowing cup, serpent on a stick, diploma, candles on a cake, skull and crossbones, a ring.

GAINING INSIGHT   30–35 minutes

Symbolic Acts
Ask a group member to read or summarize this section for the rest of the group.

Optional—The First Converts
If time permits, take a look at the testimonies of five characters from the Book of Acts. Choose five persons ahead of time to take the parts of the following characters:
❑ the Ethiopian whom Philip baptized (Acts 8:26-39)
❑ Paul (Acts 9:1-19)
❑ Cornelius (Acts 10)
❑ Lydia (Acts 16:11-15)
❑ the jailer (Acts 16:16-34)
Each should briefly tell what happened in his or her conversion and then share the witness of the immediacy of Baptism that occurred. For a more dramatic effect, each could tell his or her story in the first person and then at the end give identification. You may want to include the actual testimony of one of your group members along with these from the Acts account.

Pocket Principle

2 Enable prepared participants to move the group in the direction you've planned by stressing the focus of their sharing and the time limit allotted. Suggest each write out what he or she will say and time the reading.

Baptism
Ask a group member to read aloud Matthew 3:1-2, 6, 13-17. Then discuss the following questions:

❑ **What was required of those whom John baptized?**
(They had to repent and confess their sins.)

❑ **Why was John hesitant to baptize Jesus?** (Baptism was a sign of cleansing for sin, and John knew Jesus was without sin.)

❑ **Why then was Jesus baptized?** (It was an act of obedience to fulfill righteousness in God's sight. It also looked forward to His death and was the occasion of the affirmation of His sonship by God and the descent of the Spirit on Him.)

After a group member reads Romans 6:3-4, discuss what Baptism symbolizes for us. Note that it may represent cleansing from sin, affirmation of our new identity as a child of God, receiving the gift of the Spirit in our lives to help us live as God's child, participation in Christ's death and resurrection.

Now, read Colossians 2:11-12 aloud and discuss these questions.

❑ **What was the sign of being a part of God's chosen people in the Old Testament?** (Circumcision)

❑ **What is the sign of being a part of God's chosen people today?** (Baptism is a once-for-all event of incorporation into the body of Christ.)

❑ **What do we learn about God in the requirement of Baptism?** (That He wants us to identify ourselves with Him and with the family of God as a new creature in Christ Jesus.)

Communion
Have a group member read Luke 22:14-20. Then discuss the following questions.

❑ **List some things you can know about God from reading this passage.** (Jesus wanted to spend His last hours with His own disciples. He knew suffering was coming, but He wanted to celebrate the meaning with those into whom He had poured His life. He knew this was the first of two meals. He knew the meaning would finally be realized during kingdom experiencing. He looked at the cup and the bread, symbolizing His blood and broken body, and gave thanks. He wanted His own disciples to remember Him as they repeated this act.)

❑ **Why do you think God chose a meal instead of a message to remind us of vital truths that He didn't want us to forget?** (A meal involves many senses and that leads to remembering. It was something they could all participate in. It symbolized sustaining of life needed equally by all. It was reminiscent of the Passover celebration.)

❑ **What is God communicating to us through Communion?** (His love and obedience that caused Him to give thanks for the opportunity to provide redemption. The hope and anticipation of celebrating this event with Him in the kingdom. God desires that we regularly remember Jesus' death. Jesus' desire is to experience this with persons who believe in and follow Him.)

Have group members read 1 Corinthians 11:23-30 and discuss the following questions.

❑ **Where did Paul get his instructions about the Lord's Supper?** (What Paul wrote was written before any of the Gospels were written. That means that before there was a written record of Jesus' life, Paul was given the details and command that Christians were to celebrate this event.)

❑ **In what Old Testament celebration does Communion have its roots?** (Passover)

❑ **After Jesus took the unleavened bread, what two acts did He perform?** (He gave thanks and broke it.)

❑ **Why was the bread unleavened? What does leaven stand for in Scripture? How then is Christ like this unleavened bread?** (Leaven represented sin, so Christ was like the unleavened bread in that He contained no sin.)

❑ **How are we to receive the Lord's Supper? How are we to "remember Jesus"?** (By Jesus' acts of thanks and breaking the bread, He is symbolizing what is to take place. We are to remember His sacrifice as a personal sacrifice for us individually.)

Have group members share some things they are remembering about Jesus as they think about Him right now.

❑ **What does the cup symbolize?** (The blood of the New Covenant. The killing of an animal was a sign that a covenant agreement had been set up. Today when a young couple set up a covenant to be married they seal that promise with

127

an engagement ring. Why does that ring mean so much? The man already loved the woman before giving her the ring. He had said those loving things to her before! But the ring is a visible sign. It shows that they are committed to each other. Jesus initiated the Lord's Supper so that He might continually show His commitment to us. We receive it to show our commitment to Him. We belong to each other. The cup speaks of His covenant promise to us.)

❏ **Who are the preachers and what is proclaimed according to verse 26?** (The word used here is the same word for *preach* or *proclaim*. It is not a secret meal — but a public proclamation. We are to preach a sermon to one another about the redemptive significance of Jesus' death.

GROWING BY DOING 15–20 minutes

If your church or denomination requires the presence of an ordained person to distribute the elements of the Lord's Supper, you will want to invite the appropriate people to this session. Should the attendance of such a person be impossible, an alternative to celebrating the Supper follows.

Have group members prepare for Communion by:

Looking Back
Ask group members to share one way they have been reminded of God's mercy in this session. You may want to have prayer, sing "Let's Just Praise the Lord," "Thank You, Lord," etc. after giving a few moments to look back.

Looking In
Pause a few moments for group members to examine themselves and confess their sin to God.

Pocket Principle

2 Because some people have difficulty with silent prayer, you may want to suggest focus areas every few moments. For example: "Let's examine ourselves in relationships. In things said. In attitudes." Do not spend longer than three minutes in silent prayer.

Looking Around

Ask group members to think of ways in which we are united. Pass the bread around to each person. Some may want to say the phrase, "This is His Body for you," as they pass the bread to the next person. You may wish to sing "We Are One in the Bond of Love," "Blest Be the Tie," or "Jesus Loves Us."

Looking Forward

Pause to think of Jesus and all that awaits us on that occasion and give thanks for what you anticipate. Then have group members drink the cup, anticipating this event. Close with prayers of thanks for what it means to know God through this experience of Communion.

Optional—Alternative Response

If you choose not to celebrate Communion together, enjoy a time of worship. Use the four aspects noted above in this way:

❏ Share evidences of God's goodness and mercy.
❏ Spend time in silent confession.
❏ Find ways to express your unity—what you share together and how you are alike.
❏ Note things you anticipate when you gather with Jesus at the Marriage Supper of the Lamb.

Sing together hymns and songs that focus on the cross or on fellowship with Jesus. Some you might consider are: "Jesus Loves Us," "Let's Just Praise the Lord," "We Are One in the Bond of Love," "Blest Be the Tie," "We Exalt Thee," "We Bring the Sacrifice of Praise," "And Can It Be," "When I Survey," "Amazing Grace," "There Is Therefore Now No Condemnation," "Worthy Is the Lamb."

GOING THE SECOND MILE   5 minutes

Hymn Study

Challenge group members to reflect on the words of Charles Wesley's hymn, "And Can It Be."

GROWING AS A LEADER

Personal Assessment
What insight did you gain from your choice of **Get Acquainted** activity?

Can you recall a time when you deliberately bridged from the group's response to your next question?

What else helped to avoid the teacher-pupil answering syndrome? How did you help members to feel valued as peers and persons, not just givers of answers?

What would lead you to believe that group members feel this is their group? Do they see it as *your* group? If they do, what can you plan to do to cultivate their sense of owning the group and being a vital part of its operation?

What three words would describe how you feel about the group? Would these same words describe how you think the members feel?

What is one leadership insight you would like to plug into the next session?

SEVEN

Knowing God —
A Means to Spiritual Growth

"My . . . how you've grown!" is a very affirming state-ment for a child. "You haven't changed a bit," is sup-posed to be a compliment for an adult who hasn't been encountered for some time. But adults also change and grow. The thousands of adults who participate in continu-ing education programs every year testify to the desire adults have for change and growth to take place in their lives. In this age of technological advance and information overload, not being open to growth and change is certain obsolescence.

Because Christians see faith as "once for all, delivered to the saints," there is a danger in locking into a faith that is 20 years old and still holding. While the truths of Scripture do not change, our understanding and application of them contin-ue to grow. Five years ago we were not facing the ethical issues we face today. The same biblical truth is relevant—but our grasp of it must increase to deal with expanding horizons in our lifestyles.

Jesus expected growth among His own. His exclamation to Philip betrays His expectation: "Don't you know Me, Philip, even after I have been among you such a long time? Anyone who has seen Me has seen the Father. How can you say, 'Show us the Father'?"

In this session, we will be focusing on how knowing God fosters spiritual growth. This session will be structured a little bit differently from previous sessions. Instead of the bulk of the time being spent in the **Gaining Insight** section, the majority of time and interaction will be in the **Growing By Doing** section (which involves focusing on a scriptural passage which can be applied in each person's growing edge arenas).

As **Group Leader** of this small group experience, *you* have a choice as to which elements will best fit your group, your style of leadership, and your purposes. After you examine the **Session Objectives**, select the activities under each heading with which to begin your community building. You have many choices.

SESSION OBJECTIVES

√ To become aware of some of the factors involved in knowing God better.

√ To grow in this knowledge of God and to put into practice implications of this knowledge.

√ To actually put the process into action and grow in some aspect of the knowledge of God.

√ To enjoy studying God's Word and examine areas of our lives where we are being given opportunities to come to know God in new and more intimate ways.

GETTING ACQUAINTED   20–25 minutes

Have a group member read aloud **Knowing God—A Means to Spiritual Growth.** Then choose one of the following activities to help create a more comfortable, nonthreatening atmosphere.

Growth Report

Ask group members to respond to several of these questions with the first answer that comes to their mind.

Spiritual Growth Chart

Ask each group member to chart out his or her periods of spiritual growth since becoming a Christian. Suggest each use a line showing progression and dips, noting with a symbol or word any events, people, or other causes for peaks or valleys. Then share your chart with other group members. Impress on your group that this need not be an artistic effort but only a visual representation of times of growth. Divide into twos to share your charts or, if you wish to have the whole group exposed to each person's growth, ask each individual to select one peak or valley to share in detail.

Optional—This Is Me

To introduce the idea of growth, contact group members ahead of time and ask each to bring a baby or childhood picture of himself or herself. Collect these at the door and post them around the room with numbers. Give each person a numbered sheet to guess who's who. Call the group together after 15 minutes of observation and identify each picture.

Optional—Past Growth

Ask group members to share on each of the following questions with one other person in the group. At five-minute intervals interject the next question to be shared.

❑ A way I've seen myself grow in the past year is . . .

❑ What I remember about growing when I was a child is . . .

❑ A time I saw myself grow spiritually was when . . .

GAINING INSIGHT   30–35 minutes

The Growth Cycle

Have a group member read aloud Colossians 1:9-12. Then discuss the following questions.

❑ What format did Paul use to communicate these growth steps? (prayer for believers in Colossae)

133

❑ **What was the first thing he prayed for the Colossians?** (That they would be filled with the knowledge of God's will. He wanted them to know what God had willed.)

❑ **Where would we expect to find this revelation of God's thoughts and plans and decisions He has willed?** (Spiritual growth begins with the knowledge of God's Word, the Bible. We will never know Him unless we know His Word.)

❑ **According to verse 9, how are we to know God's will?** (In spiritual wisdom and understanding.)

❑ **Can you think of some Bible characters who knew the Word of God on an intellectual level, but didn't relate it to their lives?** (Pharisees, Ananias and Sapphira, the Corinthians who knew their bodies were temples of the Holy Spirit and yet allowed immorality in the church.)

❑ **What else did Paul pray for?** (That the Colossians would walk in a manner worthy of the Lord to please Him. The word *walk* in Scripture means daily living, lifestyle.)

❑ **How could you rephrase "live a life worthy of the Lord, pleasing Him"?** (Put God's truth into practice.)

❑ **According to this passage, what two things happen as a result of actually doing the Word of God in our lives?** (First, we bear fruit. Fruit naturally follows knowing, understanding, and responding in obedience. Second, we increase in knowing God better. In the second half of John 14:21, to the one who obeys, Jesus promises, "I will reveal myself to him.")

 GROWING BY DOING   15–20 minutes

Growing in Knowing

Divide into groups of three or four members. Have the groups read Acts 10:1-48 and apply the four steps of growth as you work through the passage together. Then instruct the small groups to discuss the questions to see what the Word means and how it can be applied to their lives.

Pocket Principle

1 If you choose to divide into groups of more than four you will need to prepare leaders ahead of time. Even with four you may want to assign groups so each is balanced with someone who will take re-

sponsibility for helping the group accomplish its purpose by the end of the time.

Know What It Says

❑ **What five or six things do you discover about Cornelius from Acts 10:1-2, 22?** (He lived in Caesarea, held rank as a centurion, and was perhaps Italian—his troops were. His whole family was religious, practicing what they believed. He was generous, supplying the poor, and he had a regular prayer life.)

❑ **What was a centurion?** (A Roman army officer in charge of 100 men.)

❑ **What was unusual about Cornelius being a "God-fearing" man?** (He served Rome, a non-God-fearing nation. He didn't seem to have any outside encouragement to honor God.)

❑ **Considering his job, why would it be unique to be respected by the Jews?** (Normally Jews hated the Roman oppressors, especially the army enforcers of Roman law.)

❑ **What started Cornelius' learning experience?** (In the midst of prayer, he had a vision of an angel of God.

❑ **Keeping in mind how God began Cornelius' lesson, how does verse 9 suggest God began Peter's lesson?** (With Peter praying and then falling into a trance.)

Understand the Meaning

❑ **Describe God's lesson for Peter in your own words.** (The Gospel is for all, not just Jews. Gentiles are open to its message and are valued by God who wants them to become His children also.)

❑ **Why didn't Peter understand? Why did God use a vision to teach him?** (When God wants to change deep-seated protected attitudes, He often puts truth in a new form so it isn't rejected immediately. Recall Nathan's method in confronting David's sin.)

❑ **What did Peter understand?** (Jewish law didn't allow personal association with Gentiles, but God has no prejudice against them.)

❑ **Who helped Peter find the truth?** (God used Cornelius to illustrate His truth.)

❑ **In what ways did Peter respond to the lesson even though he didn't totally understand its meaning?** (He

135

invited Gentiles into his house, he entered a Gentile house, and he went with Gentiles without objecting.)

❏ **How did Cornelius show he was teachable?** (He immediately obeyed the first step given to him. He gathered those important to him to hear new truth. He believed Peter was under God's command and was open to listening.)

❏ **How did Peter show he was teachable?** (He obeyed as commanded by God. He admitted being shown new truth by God and learning something new about God.)

❏ **Scan verses 34-43 to find what lessons Peter learned and what lessons he taught.** (God doesn't show favoritism in receiving person. He responds to those who honor and obey. Peace through Jesus is God's message to Israel. Jesus is Lord of all. God was with Jesus in the Person of the Spirit and in power. Jesus healed because of God's divine power. Jews killed Jesus, but God brought Him to life. Select believers including His disciples saw Him in resurrected form. We are commanded to preach and testify that He is to be Judge. The prophets declared forgiveness of sins to everyone who believes in Him.)

❏ **What were the results of these two older, experienced, successful, respected men being open to learn from God at this time in their lives? How were they affected by what they learned? Who else was affected by what they learned?** (Gentiles received the Spirit and responded as did the Jews at Pentecost. Gentiles were baptized. The apostles and believers in Judea learned that God wanted to save Gentiles too.)

Encourage group members to spend as much time as necessary working through and sharing their responses to the remaining questions in **How It Works in Our Lives** and **Start Doing It.**

After the smaller groups have finished, reassemble the whole group and ask volunteers to share how they were affected by what they learned in Acts. Rejoice over these insights that lead to growth.

You may want to close by singing "What a Mighty God Is He" (or some hymn that focuses on God's ability), committing ourselves to the One who is able to change us and our world.

GOING THE SECOND MILE   5 minutes

Group Checkup
Challenge group members to complete this section on their own as they consider who they will encourage to pursue spiritual growth.

GROWING AS A LEADER

Personal Assessment
Consider the following questions as you evaluate this session.

What principles would you share with a new group leader about putting members in groups and helping them get the most out of that time?

Who in our group has the potential for leading a small group? What causes you to think this person has that potential? How could you begin to involve this person in shared leadership in the group?

Are you able to list some area of growth seen in each group member over the course of our meeting together? How could you express this to each one to affirm them and to encourage them to go on growing?

Where do you see the group still needing to grow?

EIGHT

Knowing God in Celebration

"You are invited . . ." usually signals the announcement of some form of celebration. In this session, we are joining together to celebrate who God is and what He has done in our midst. It is a time of reflection and joy as we recount His goodness and remember His acts in our lives.

Celebration was no stranger to Israel. The people of God were enjoined to keep certain holidays in which they recalled (on a yearly basis) what God had done. They were to keep alive for future generations the memory and praise that had been present at the first celebration. Israel's expressions of joy included feasting and fasting, dancing and song, meditation and worship.

What better place to celebrate our God than among those who have pursued God with us and have shown us His likeness. You may wish to set up a party atmosphere for this small group session or begin with a meal to indicate that this is a festive affair.

As **Group Leader** of this small group experience, *you* have a choice as to which elements will best fit your group, your style of leadership, and your purposes. After you examine the **Session Objectives**, select the activities under each heading with which to begin your community building. You have many choices.

GETTING ACQUAINTED   20–25 minutes

Have a group member read aloud **Celebrate!** Then choose one of the following activities to help create a more comfortable, nonthreatening atmosphere.

Planning My Own Party
Ask group members to share how they would plan a celebration party.

Optional—Have a Good Time
Ask group members if they could do anything to enjoy themselves, what would it be? This need not be limited to what they could realistically do. Dreams and fantasy activities are allowed. Ask each good time celebrant to write the chosen enjoyable activity on a piece of paper. Collect the papers and read them aloud, asking members to guess the identity of the people who wrote them.

Optional—Remember When
Invite group members to select a period of time or a peak experience from life to share, basing their selections on the criteria of "I see this as an especially good time in my life." Ask: **What made it such a good time? How was God a part of this good time? Would you like to experience this event or time period again? Why or why not?**

Optional — God Having a Good Time

J.B. Phillips once wrote a book, *Your God Is Too Small* (Macmillan, 1953), emphasizing the limitations we place on our concept of God. He found that during World War II, young people in England believed that God could create the universe but that He probably couldn't comprehend radar, which at that time was a new concept. Discuss the following questions:

❏ When you think of God having a good time, what picture comes to mind?

❏ What does God do to express joy?

❏ Describe the concepts of God and good times that have developed and accumulated in your mind over the years.

GAINING INSIGHT   30–35 minutes

Scripture Study

Take turns reading aloud Luke 15:11-32. Then discuss the following questions.

❏ What was the setting for this celebration? (Home with father, brother, and servants.)

❏ What prompted this celebration? (Homecoming of a wayward son.)

❏ What elements were planned for the party? (Festive garment, jewelry, new shoes, food, music, and dancing.)

Have group members share what they would say if they were one of the characters at this party.

❏ What were the actions of the father in celebration? (He ran to his son, hugged and kissed him. He commanded the servants to bring gifts for his son. He gave orders for the choicest of food, called for a party, and went out to reconcile with the older brother.)

❏ What were the father's attitudes in His joy? (Compassion, acceptance, generosity, patience, and reasonableness.)

140

❑ **What do the father's words tell us about his character?** (He was forgiving and forgetting—he never brought up the past. He was gracious, aware of his son's needs, just, free to express his feelings, not vengeful or reserved, lavished love, in charge, generous. He lived with no regrets, focused on the positive and the present.)

❑ **What can we learn about God from the good time pictured here?** (God initiates good times. He expresses His joy with vigor. He celebrates the positive joyous moment without reminding us of negatives of the past. God meets our needs so we have fullness of joy. He expects others to join in His joy. He finds joy in our obedience to the truth. He cares for those who may misunderstand our celebration, and He wants to be a part of our good times.)

Ask group members to share which of these findings is particularly significant for them personally.

❑ **What do we learn about the other characters involved in celebration?** (The younger son felt ashamed and not worthy, but he took responsibility for his actions and the results. The older son exhibited anger, jealousy, and self-pity. He felt self-righteous and negatively evaluated his brother. The servants expedited the father's commands as well as informed the older brother of this incident.)

Encourage group members to share some good times where God was the center of their praise.

GROWING BY DOING   15–20 minutes

Praise Him
Ask a group member to read aloud Psalm 111. Note that the psalmist says he will praise God in the midst of God's people. Have group members list significant things that have happened in our group—something we learned, answers to prayer, development of new relationships, etc. that we can celebrate in praise.

You may choose to spend time going over your list and offering specific praise in prayer as you celebrate or you can add a

141

fresh touch to celebration by dividing into groups to write brief psalms of praise incorporating items mentioned as good. Follow the format of Psalm 111 or Psalms 100, 103, 105, or 118. Encourage each group to include specifics that are important to them. A simple way to write such a psalm is to state God's characteristic and list ways that it has been evidenced in the lives of the people. For example, "The works of your hands are faithful and just; You provided a job for Elaine when she didn't know where to turn." Or, "Your words are trustworthy and revealing. We have seen You to be a God who keeps His promise to be among us and to cause us to love each other." When finished, the sharing of these group psalms is a fitting climactic celebration to eight weeks of knowing God.

Allow at least 20 minutes for each group to compose their psalm with items significant to them. Then celebrate by reading them as your group's praise.

Pocket Principle

1 **A sense of closure is vital to a good group experience. There needs to be awareness that all issues have been handled. If you sense any hurt, misunderstanding, or opposition among members of the group, make time for these to be brought out in the open and give freedom to evaluate and heal.**

Optional—Worship Ideas
Worship may occur in the recital of thanksgiving for the highlights of your group or in the sharing of the psalms. Should you desire an extended time of focusing on the God you have come to know during this session, select a few of the following songs and/or ask volunteers to share what they have come to know about God. Compile a list of insights and give praise with a clap offering or cheer.

Songs of celebration might include: "Holy, Holy, Holy," "When Morning Gilds the Skies," "Clap Your Hands," "Doxology," "Come Into His Presence," "Great Is Thy Faithfulness," "O Come Let Us Adore Him," "He Has Made Me Glad," "Praise the Name of Jesus," "Come Let Us Offer the Sacrifice of Praise."

GOING THE SECOND MILE   5 minutes

Celebrate You
Challenge group members to write a celebration note to a person or to the group expressing their joy over them.

GROWING AS A LEADER

Congratulations!
You have led this group through numerous growing experiences and helped them grapple with the highest of priorities—that of knowing God. This is a great time to take stock of what you as a leader have learned over the past eight sessions.

Use some of the tools below to help you think through growth and skill development. For maximum benefit share your answers with another person who knows you well and has been in your group. You may want several in the group to give you feedback on the items below so you get a balanced perspective and broader insight.

In what ways were you satisfied with the results of this group?

How do you feel about the style of leadership you supplied?

❑ Highly pleased with

❑ Need to grow in

❑ Learned how to

❑ Need equipping in how to

What is something you learned about being in a small group?

143

What is something you would do differently next time?

Circle the number which best indicates your response.

To what extent do you feel members learned to love and care for one another?

0   1   2   3   4   5   6   7   8   9   10

Remained Individualistic   High Care and Concern

To what extent do you feel members learned something new about the subject and about each other?

0   1   2   3   4   5   6   7   8   9   10

Remained Same   High Learning

How well did group members show support and acceptance of individuals? How was this evidenced?

0   1   2   3   4   5   6   7   8   9   10

Very Low   Very High

To what extent did group members grow and show change?

0   1   2   3   4   5   6   7   8   9   10

Extremely Low   Very High

How satisfied were members with their group experience?

0   1   2   3   4   5   6   7   8   9   10

Dissatisfied   Very Satisfied

To what extent were your goals fulfilled in leading a group?

0   1   2   3   4   5   6   7   8   9   10

Unfulfilled   Fulfilled